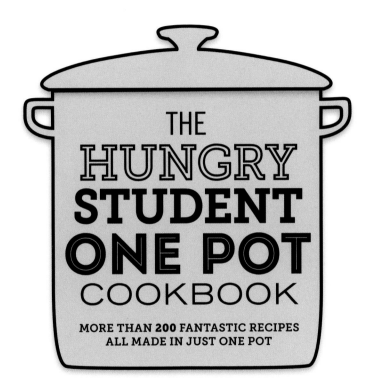

THE
HUNGRY
STUDENT
ONE POT
COOKBOOK

**MORE THAN 200 FANTASTIC RECIPES
ALL MADE IN JUST ONE POT**

spruce

An Hachette UK Company
www.hachette.co.uk

First published in Great Britain in 2017 by Spruce,
a division of Octopus Publishing Group Ltd,
Carmelite House, 50 Victoria Embankment,
London EC4Y 0DZ
www.octopusbooks.co.uk
www.octopusbooksusa.com

Copyright © Octopus Publishing Group 2017

Distributed in the US by Hachette Book Group,
1290 Avenue of the Americas, 4th and 5th Floors,
New York, NY 10020

Distributed in Canada by Canadian Manda Group,
664 Annette St., Toronto, Ontario,
Canada M6S 2C8

ISBN 978-1-84601-542-7

A CIP catalogue record for this book is available
from the British Library

Printed and bound in China

10 9 8 7 6 5 4 3 2 1

The recipes in this book have been labelled as
suitable for vegan and vegetarian diets.
Vegetarians should look for the 'V' symbol on
a cheese to ensure it is made with vegetarian
rennet. There are vegetarian forms of Parmesan,
feta, Cheddar, Cheshire, Red Leicester, dolcelatte
and many goats' cheeses, among others.

Standard level spoon measurement are used
in all recipes.
1 tablespoon = one 15 ml spoon
1 teaspoon = one 5 ml spoon

Ovens should be preheated to the specific
temperature—if using a fan-assisted oven, follow
manufacturer's instructions for adjusting the
time and the temperature.

Recipes that require these special appliances
are indicated with the below icons.

**FOOD
PROCESSOR**   **MICROWAVE**   **SLOW
COOKER**

Contents

INTRODUCTION

When you move out of home for the first time, hopefully you will have gleaned enough skills to enable you to wash your own clothes, find your way around campus, and cook yourself a decent meal. That doesn't mean you need to have perfected the culinary arts but being able to rustle up a passable dinner and expand your repertoire beyond toast and cereal will make mealtimes far more enjoyable.

Cooking everything in one dish is less daunting than having to master a number of different skills and, even if you don't have much experience in the kitchen beyond boiling the kettle or slicing cheese for sandwiches, you should soon be able to create a variety of healthy and tasty meals that will help to keep your limited budget in check.

One-pot cooking minimizes preparation time and washing up, which is good news for anyone who doesn't want to spend hours in the kitchen but still wants to enjoy a home-cooked meal in the evening. It also reduces waste, as many recipes are adaptable—particularly stews and casseroles where you can chuck in any old vegetables and herbs that happen to be lying around, rather than consigning them to the garbage. One-pot cooking also conserves energy because you're not using every ring on the stove, or keeping the oven and stove running at the same time for lengthy periods of time. Plus, a slow cooker uses less energy than an electric oven, even when it has been on for 6 or 7 hours.

KITCHEN EQUIPMENT

Whether you're moving into student accommodation or a shared house, you'll need to bring a certain amount of utensils and equipment with you in order to prepare and cook food. It makes sense to put together a list of what you'll need and divide it up between you and your housemates before moving-in day. That way, you won't end up with a pantry full of lemon squeezers and garlic crushers but only enough plates and cutlery for two people to eat dinner together.

It's unlikely that you'll be able to afford to splash out on fancy gadgets and designer crockery and there's really no need—between wear and tear, accidents and neglect, the contents of a student kitchen will be put through their paces. However, one-pot cooking means you'll be relying on a large pan, casserole, and probably another oven-to-table pot—and it's worth spending a little more to buy a couple of pieces of quality cookware that will stay the distance.

ESSENTIAL UTENSILS AND EQUIPMENT

- **Sharp knives** Two good knives should cover all your needs—a large one for meat and fish and a smaller one for paring and cutting vegetables.
- **Utensils** Measuring cups, two mixing bowls, wooden spoon, rolling pin, grater, spatula, cutting board, vegetable peeler, whisk, colander.
- **Handheld blender** You can buy a handheld blender for a few dollars and you'll find this really useful for making soups and sauces.

SLOW COOKER

A number of the recipes in this book are prepared and cooked in a slow cooker. It's worth investing in one as you can use it to cook healthy, hearty meals with the minimum of effort. And if you thought slow cookers were all about casseroles, think again—you can prepare everything from pot-roast chicken to curry and even sponge puddings in them, so they're extremely versatile.

You can buy a good-quality, large-capacity slow cooker for under $40, which is great value, considering the time and money you'll save once you get into the habit of using it regularly. Choose a brand name that you trust and check out online reviews before you decide which one to buy. If you're planning on cooking meals for your housemates, or you want to make extra portions to freeze, then size matters—choose a slow cooker with a capacity of 5-6 quarts. It's also worth checking that it includes a timer, so it will stop cooking and just keep the food warm if you're away from home.

SLOW COOKER TIPS

- Clean the cooker as soon as possible after use so food doesn't dry solid. Always unplug the slow cooker before cleaning it.
- Don't add extra liquid to the cooker, unless stated in the recipe. The tight-fitting lid stops any liquid from evaporating so the food will stay moist.
- Keep the lid on during cooking—it might be tempting to take a quick peek inside but you'll tamper with the temperature if you do.
- Brown meat in a skillet before adding it to the slow cooker. Okay, so that's not technically one-pot cooking but it's all in the name of flavor.

PANTRY *staples*

One-pot cookery is perfectly suited to long and slow cooking and you'll need a pantry full of healthy grains and pulses, as well as a good selection of fresh ingredients, plus herbs and spices to add depth of flavor to your meals.

- **Salt and pepper** Fine salt and ground pepper are ideal for seasoning dishes, while sea salt and freshly ground pepper make a sophisticated addition to the dinner table.
- **Oil** Vegetable oil is a good everyday option for cooking and olive oil is perfect for salad dressings, marinades, and sauces.
- **Canned chopped tomatoes** Essential for sauces, soups, and stews, this is a cheap and nutritious ingredient that you can buy in bulk.

- **Onions and garlic** These two ingredients are essential in many cuisines and they form the base for a lot of savory dishes in this book. Make sure you have a steady supply of both onions and garlic in the kitchen.
- **Rice** There are lots of different varieties of rice. You'll need arborio rice if you want to cook risottos and jasmine rice for Thai food. Brown rice is the healthy option but it takes longer to cook so take this into account when you're planning your meals. Pick a couple of the rice varieties that you think you'll use most often and buy in bulk.
- **Pasta** Again, choose just a couple of large packages of the pasta shapes you think you will use most frequently so you don't end up with dozens of different types of pasta filling up your pantry. Pasta is a student staple and is well suited to one-pot cooking so you'll be eating a lot of it.
- **Cans of beans** Stock up on cheap, protein-rich varieties like kidney beans (great for chilis), borlotti, and lima beans (ideal for adding bulk to soups) and chickpeas (perfect for stews, curries, and salads.)
- **Lentils** Healthy, nutritious, and incredibly cheap, what's not to like about lentils? Red lentils break down when they are cooked for a long time, which makes them really useful for thickening up soups and stews. French Puy lentils hold their shape and are delicious in confits and casseroles.

Meal planning & shopping lists

You'll save a lot of money on your food bill if you plan your meals in advance. By shopping for exactly what you need for each meal, you'll reduce food wastage and avoid costly impulse buys. It only takes a few minutes to work out a rough plan for the week's meals. Cooking together as a household will also save money but it does mean that you'll need to be a bit more organized and get everyone together to agree on the weekly meal plan, cooking rota, and food shop.

Don't worry if you can't stick to the plan rigidly—things will crop up during the week, which means people heading out at the last minute, or bringing friends home for dinner. Luckily, one-pot cooking is pretty flexible when it comes to working around a student lifestyle and an extra person at the dinner table shouldn't put a spanner in the works. Likewise, one less for dinner means an extra portion that you can store in the refrigerator or freezer to be eaten another time.

Once you've worked out a rough plan for the week, it makes sense to do one large grocery shop for all the main ingredients, plus other essentials that you'll need like milk, bread, cereal, and fruit. If you don't have a car and don't fancy heaving a week's worth of food for a house full of hungry students on the bus, then online shopping is definitely the most convenient way to buy your groceries. Inevitably, there'll be extras required during the week and a little blackboard or notebook in the kitchen is a handy way to keep track of what's needed. That way, whoever is passing the shops can top off when they go out.

VARIETY IS THE SPICE OF LIFE

When you're planning your meals, take into account any dietary requirements, likes, and dislikes so that everyone has a say in the week's menu. Alternatively, if there is a mix of vegetarians and meat-eaters, it might make more sense to prepare different meals. However you organize the cooking and planning, try to include a good variety of meals to keep dinnertime interesting. So, for example:

- **Monday:** casserole–try the Mixed Seafood Casserole (page 145) or Mustardy Squash, Carrot & Sweet Potato Casserole (page 152).
- **Tuesday:** rice dish–try the Bacon, Pea & Zucchini Risotto (page 94) or Pork & Tomato Rice Pot (page 131).
- **Wednesday:** veggie meal–try the Veggie Bean Chili (page 113) or Brown Rice, Mint & Haloumi Pilaf (page 153).
- **Thursday:** Italian night–try the Pizza Fiorentina (page 49) or Spicy Tuna, Tomato & Olive Pasta (page 106).
- **Friday:** fish supper–try the Crispy Fish Pie (page 138) or Oven-Baked Fish & Chips with Tomato Salsa (page 144).
- **Saturday:** curry–try the Pea & Lamb Korma (page 137) or Chicken & Caramelized Onion Dhal (page 170).
- **Sunday:** meat lover's Sunday lunch–try the Roast Chicken with Butternut Squash (page 72) or Spicy Pulled Ham with Apricots (page 177).

HOW TO USE THIS BOOK

Each recipe in the book can be prepared and cooked in just one dish–whether that's a slow cooker, casserole, saucepan, ovenproof dish, or a bowl in the microwave. There is also a number of cold dishes and salads that don't require any cooking at all –all you have to do is mix the ingredients together and serve.

In addition to the one dish, you will also need a few basic kitchen utensils to cook the recipes (see Essential Utensils & Equipment, page 5), and occasionally a recipe will call for a kitchen appliance, such as a microwave, food processor, or slow cooker–we've flagged any recipes that need one of these appliances so that they are easy to spot.

Most of the ingredients you need are everyday items that are not costly or difficult to source, though we have included a few more unusual recipes for special occasions and for when you become more confident and creative in the kitchen.

To help you keep within your food budget, each recipe in this book is rated from 1 to 3, with 1s providing end-of-term saviors that can be scraped together for a pittance, and 3s to splash out and impress all your friends.

WHAT'S FOR LUNCH?

PAELLA SOUP

MASALA DHAL & SWEET POTATO

MINTED PEA SOUP

FEEL-GOOD *broth*

2 boneless, skinless chicken
  breasts, about 10 oz in total
3½ cups cold chicken stock
  (see page 11 for homemade)
1 lemon slice
2 teaspoons coarsely chopped
  thyme
8 oz fresh meat cappelletti or
  small tortellini
salt and pepper
grated Parmesan cheese,
  to serve

Serves **4**
Prep time **5 minutes**
Cooking time **25 minutes**

1 Put the chicken breasts, stock, lemon slice, and thyme
in a large saucepan. Bring to a very gentle simmer—the
water should shiver rather than bubble in the pan.
Cover and cook for 15-16 minutes until the chicken is
opaque all the way through. Remove and discard the
lemon slice.

2 Lift the chicken from the liquid with a slotted spoon
and transfer to a plate. When the chicken is cool
enough to handle, shred into large pieces.

3 Bring the stock to a rapid boil and season with salt and
pepper. Add the pasta and cook for 2-3 minutes, adding
the shredded chicken for the last minute of the
cooking time. Serve immediately with a generous
sprinkling of grated Parmesan.

VARIATION
For a chicken broth with egg, beat 2 eggs well. Follow
the recipe above, removing the soup from the heat
once the pasta is cooked and gradually pouring in the
eggs in a steady stream, stirring as you go. Sprinkle
with 2 tablespoons chopped tarragon and serve.

AFFORDABILITY
1

CHICKEN MULLIGATAWNY

1 Melt half the butter in a saucepan and fry the chicken thighs in two batches for 5 minutes each, until golden on all sides. Lift out with a slotted spoon onto a plate.

2 Add the remaining butter and fry the onions, carrots, and apple, stirring, for 6–8 minutes until lightly browned.

3 Sprinkle in the flour and cook, stirring, for 1 minute. Gradually blend in the stock, then stir in the curry paste, tomato paste, and rice. Return the chicken to the pan and bring to a simmer, stirring. Reduce the heat, cover, and cook very gently for 1 hour, or until the chicken is cooked through and very tender.

4 Lift the chicken pieces from the soup with a slotted spoon and transfer to a plate. Once cool enough to handle, pull the meat from the bones. Shred half the meat into pieces and return the remainder to the pan. Blend the soup using a handheld blender.

5 Return the shredded chicken to the pan and heat through. Season to taste with salt and pepper. Ladle the soup into serving bowls and serve topped with spoonfuls of yogurt.

COOKING TIP

For a homemade chicken stock, place 1 large chicken carcass or 1 lb chicken bones in a large saucepan and add 2 halved, unpeeled onions, 2 coarsely chopped carrots, 1 coarsely chopped celery stalk, several bay leaves, and 1 teaspoon black or white peppercorns. Just cover with cold water and bring to a gentle simmer. Reduce the heat to its lowest setting and cook, uncovered, for 2 hours. Strain through a fine strainer and let cool. Cover and store in the refrigerator for up to several days or freeze for up to 6 months.

3½ tablespoons butter
1 lb 3 oz bone-in, skinless chicken thighs
2 onions, chopped
2 small carrots, chopped
1 small cooking apple, peeled, cored, and chopped
1 tablespoon all-purpose flour
4 cups chicken stock (see tip for homemade)
2 tablespoons mild curry paste
2 tablespoons tomato paste
¼ cup basmati rice
salt and pepper
plain yogurt, to serve

Serves **6**
Prep time **20 minutes**
Cooking time **1½ hours**

Spicy CHICKEN SOUP
WITH AVOCADO

2 tablespoons olive oil
1 onion, chopped
3 garlic cloves, crushed
1 teaspoon chipotle peppers
  in adobo sauce, chopped,
  or Tabasco sauce
2 teaspoons sugar
13 oz can chopped tomatoes
4 cups hot chicken stock (see
  page 11 for homemade)
2 ready-cooked chicken
  breasts, torn into strips
1 ripe avocado, peeled, pitted,
  and cubed
handful of tortilla chips,
  crushed
4 tablespoons sour cream
handful of chopped cilantro
salt and pepper

Serves **4**
Prep time **20 minutes**
Cooking time **20 minutes**

1 Heat the oil in a large saucepan. Add the onion and cook for 5 minutes until softened, then stir in the garlic, chipotle peppers or Tabasco sauce, and sugar. Pour in the tomatoes and stock, bring to a boil, then reduce the heat and simmer for 10 minutes.

2 Use a handheld blender to puree the soup until smooth, then add a little boiling water if it is too thick and season to taste with salt and pepper.

3 Ladle the soup into serving bowls and sprinkle the chicken, avocado and tortilla chips on top. Drizzle with the sour cream and sprinkle with the chopped cilantro.

VARIATION
For a spicy chicken and avocado salad, mix a few drops of Tabasco sauce with ½ teaspoon ground cumin and 1 tablespoon olive oil in a bowl. Coat 2 chicken breast fillets, cut into strips, in the oil. Cook the chicken in a hot griddle pan for 3 minutes on each side, or until cooked through. In a large bowl, toss together 3½ oz mixed salad greens, 2 chopped tomatoes, 1 sliced avocado, the chicken, some crushed tortilla chips, the juice of ½ lime, and 1 tablespoon olive oil.

AFFORDABILITY 2

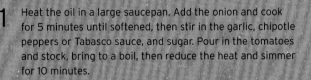

EASY CHICKEN PHO

3 cups chicken stock (see page 11 for homemade)
1 shallot, chopped
2 garlic cloves, finely chopped
½ oz piece of fresh ginger root, peeled and chopped
¼ teaspoon dried red pepper flakes
1 tablespoon dark soy sauce
1 teaspoon Thai fish sauce
7 oz boneless, skinless chicken breast, cut into small pieces
2 oz instant rice noodles
1⅓ cups bean sprouts

To garnish
2 scallions, thinly sliced
chopped cilantro

Serves **2**
Prep time **10 minutes**
Cooking time **20 minutes**

1 Put the stock, shallot, garlic, ginger, red pepper flakes, soy sauce, and fish sauce in a saucepan and bring to a gentle simmer, making sure the liquid doesn't boil. Cover and cook very gently for 10 minutes to infuse the flavors.

2 Add the chicken to the pan, stir well, and cook gently for 5 minutes. Add the rice noodles and cook for another 4-5 minutes, stirring frequently, until the noodles are tender.

3 Stir in the bean sprouts and cook for a few seconds until heated through. Divide between 2 serving bowls and garnish with the scallions and chopped cilantro.

CHICKEN CORN
Chowder

1. Place the creamed corn in a saucepan with the milk and heat, stirring.

2. Add the chicken, corn kernels, and scallions and season with salt and pepper. Simmer for 5 minutes, stirring occasionally.

3. Blend the cornstarch with 1 tablespoon water in a mug, pour into the soup, and stir to thicken. Ladle the soup into serving bowls and serve with crusty bread.

VARIATION
For a chicken, bacon, and corn chowder, fry 2 chopped slices of bacon with 1 chopped onion and 2 chopped potatoes in a little butter for 5 minutes. Pour in 2 cups milk and simmer for 10 minutes. Stir in generous 2/3 cup frozen corn kernels and 6 oz chopped ready-cooked chicken. Season to taste with salt and pepper, heat through, and serve sprinkled with chopped parsley.

11 oz can creamed corn
generous 1¾ cups milk
6 oz ready-cooked chicken, torn
 into pieces
generous ¾ cup frozen corn
 kernels
2 scallions, chopped
2 teaspoons cornstarch
salt and pepper
crusty bread, to serve

Serves **4**
Prep time **5 minutes**
Cooking time **10 minutes**

MASALA DHAL
& SWEET POTATO

1 Heat the oil in a saucepan and fry the onions for 5 minutes. Add the garlic, red pepper flakes, ginger, garam masala, and turmeric and cook, stirring, for 2 minutes.

2 Add the split peas, tomatoes, and 3 cups of the stock and bring to a boil. Reduce the heat, cover, and cook gently for 20 minutes, or until the peas have started to soften, adding more stock if the mixture runs dry.

3 Stir in the sweet potatoes, cover again, and cook for another 20 minutes, or until the potatoes and peas are tender, adding more stock if necessary to keep the dhal juicy. Tip the spinach into the pan and stir until wilted. Add a little salt to taste. Serve with warm naan breads and mango chutney.

COOKING TIP
For homemade vegetable stock, heat 1 tablespoon vegetable oil in a large saucepan and gently fry 2 unpeeled and coarsely chopped onions, 2 each coarsely chopped carrots, celery stalks, parsnips, and zucchini, and scant 3 cups trimmed and sliced mushrooms, stirring frequently, for 10 minutes, or until softened. Add 3 bay leaves and a handful of parsley and thyme sprigs. Pour in 6⅓ cups cold water and bring to a boil. Reduce the heat and simmer very gently, uncovered, for 40 minutes. Strain through a strainer and cool. Cover and store in the refrigerator for up to several days or freeze for up to 6 months.

3 tablespoons vegetable oil
2 onions, chopped
2 garlic cloves, crushed
½ teaspoon dried red pepper flakes
¾ inch piece of fresh ginger root, peeled and grated
2 teaspoons garam masala
½ teaspoon ground turmeric
1½ cups dried split yellow peas, rinsed and drained
7 oz can chopped tomatoes
4 cups vegetable stock (see tip for homemade)
1 lb sweet potatoes, scrubbed and cut into small chunks
4 cups spinach, washed and drained
salt

To serve
warm naan breads
mango chutney

Serves **4**
Prep time **15 minutes**
Cooking time **50 minutes**

AFFORDABILITY
1

PESTO LEMON SOUP

1 tablespoon olive oil
1 onion, finely chopped
2 garlic cloves, finely chopped
2 tomatoes, skinned (see tip)
    and chopped
5 cups vegetable stock (see
    page 15 for homemade)
1 tablespoon store-bought fresh
    green pesto, plus extra to
    serve
grated zest and juice of 1 lemon
3½ oz broccoli, cut into small
    florets and stems sliced
5 oz zucchini, diced
1 cup frozen podded soybeans
½ cup small dried pasta shapes
1 cup spinach, washed, drained,
    and shredded
salt and pepper
basil leaves, to garnish
    (optional)
olive or sundried tomato
    focaccia or ciabatta, to serve

Serves **6**
Prep time **10 minutes**
Cooking time **25 minutes**

1 Heat the oil in a saucepan and gently fry the onion for 5 minutes, or until softened. Add the garlic, tomatoes, stock, pesto, lemon zest, and a little salt and pepper and simmer gently for 10 minutes.

2 Add the broccoli, zucchini, soybeans, and pasta shapes and simmer for 6 minutes.

3 Stir the spinach and lemon juice into the pan and cook for 2 minutes, or until the spinach has just wilted and the pasta is just tender.

4 Ladle the soup into serving bowls, top with extra spoonfuls of pesto, and garnish with a few basil leaves, if desired. Serve with olive or sundried tomato focaccia or ciabatta.

COOKING TIP

Tomato skins don't soften, even when cooked for some time, so are worth removing. Pull away the stalks, make a slit with a knife, and place the tomatoes in a heatproof bowl. Cover with boiling water and let stand for about 30 seconds if the tomatoes are very ripe, or a couple of minutes if very firm. Drain and fill the bowl with cold water. Peel away the skins and halve or chop the tomatoes as required.

AFFORDABILITY
1

PAELLA SOUP

AFFORDABILITY 2

1 Heat the oil in a large heavy saucepan. Add the chorizo and onion and cook for 2 minutes, or until the onion has softened and the chorizo is lightly browned.

2 Stir in the garlic, then add the tomatoes, stock, and saffron, and season to taste with salt and pepper. Bring to a boil, add the chicken and red pepper, and simmer for 10-12 minutes, or until the chicken is cooked through.

3 Add the rice and peas and cook for 2-3 minutes until heated through. Ladle the soup into serving bowls.

1 tablespoon olive oil
8 oz chorizo sausage, chopped
1 onion, finely chopped
2 garlic cloves, crushed
7 oz can chopped tomatoes
4 cups chicken stock (see page 11 for homemade)
pinch of saffron threads
2 skinless chicken breast fillets, cubed
1 red bell pepper, cored, seeded, and chopped
2 cups ready-cooked rice
scant ½ cup frozen peas, defrosted
salt and pepper

Serves **4**
Prep time **15 minutes**
Cooking time **25 minutes**

CHICKPEA & RED PEPPER SOUP

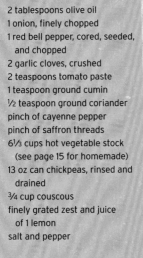

2 tablespoons olive oil
1 onion, finely chopped
1 red bell pepper, cored, seeded,
   and chopped
2 garlic cloves, crushed
2 teaspoons tomato paste
1 teaspoon ground cumin
½ teaspoon ground coriander
pinch of cayenne pepper
pinch of saffron threads
6⅓ cups hot vegetable stock
   (see page 15 for homemade)
13 oz can chickpeas, rinsed and
   drained
¾ cup couscous
finely grated zest and juice
   of 1 lemon
salt and pepper

To garnish
handful of chopped mint
handful of chopped cilantro

Serves **4**
Prep time **15 minutes**
Cooking time **20 minutes**

1 Heat the oil in a large heavy saucepan. Add the onion and cook for 5 minutes, then add the red bell pepper, garlic, tomato paste, and spices and cook for another 1 minute.

2 Pour in the stock and bring to a boil, then reduce the heat and simmer for 5 minutes. Add the chickpeas and simmer for another 5 minutes, then season to taste with salt and pepper.

3 Add the couscous and a squeeze of lemon juice and cook for 1 minute, or until the couscous is tender. Ladle into serving bowls and garnish with the chopped herbs and grated lemon zest.

VARIATION

For a chickpea and red bell pepper couscous, heat 1 tablespoon olive oil in a large heavy saucepan. Add 2 sliced garlic cloves and cook for 1 minute, then add 1 chopped ready-roasted pepper, 7 oz canned chickpeas, rinsed and drained, and 1⅓ cups couscous. Remove from the heat. Pour in generous 1 cup hot vegetable stock, cover, and leave for 5 minutes until tender. Stir in a good squeeze of lemon juice and 3 oz arugula.

AFFORDABILITY 1

EAT WELL FOR LESS

It's the age-old student conundrum—how do you eat well on a meager budget that is already taking the strain of other important commitments like beer, gig nights ... oh, and books. Well luckily, one-pot meals are perfectly suited to upcycling humble everyday fare into incredible dishes that will please your wallet and your taste buds. And, when you do find you have a few spare cents in your purse, you can splash out on more extravagant ingredients for special occasions.

BUDGET

Before you can start planning what you're going to cook and eat, you need to be aware of exactly how much you have to spend on food. That means looking at your total income and taking off the cost of your rent, bills, and other recurring overheads and seeing what's left. You can do this on a monthly or weekly basis and either set aside a specific amount for food, or you can decide each week what you can realistically spend.

Next you need to decide if you're shopping individually, or clubbing together with your housemates. The good thing about buying your food together is that you can take advantage of bulk buys and discounts; the downside is that the kitchen pantry can end up becoming a bit of a free-for-all, and you won't have exclusive ownership rights to the last slab of cheese or your favorite box of cereal.

SHOP AROUND

Once you've worked out your budget and food sharing arrangements, it's time to work out where you can get the most for your money. If you have more than one grocery store close by, you can try price comparison websites to ensure you're paying the cheapest price for your regular items. Indoor and outdoor markets which have fruit and veg stalls can offer very good value for money. Plus, if you loiter around the stalls toward the end of the day, you'll find vendors offering massive discounts to clear their stock. Likewise, farmers' markets are worth a trip for good quality seasonal produce. Online shopping can save you time and money—many grocery store offer free delivery slots at unpopular times (which can work to your advantage as a student).

Don't be tempted by unrealistic offers— will you really work your way through two cartons of peaches in a day?

Pick up bargains at the end of the day and tuck them away in your freezer— this is a great option for meat and fish, which can be expensive.

Don't be afraid to shop around and buy different ingredients from different stores or market stalls.

Nothing beats a Saturday takeout curry or Chinese meal but with a little practice and not much effort you can make your own versions for a fraction of the cost.

Minted PEA SOUP (V)

1 tablespoon butter
1 onion, finely chopped
1 potato, finely chopped
4 cups vegetable stock (see
   page 15 for homemade)
scant 3¼ cups frozen peas
6 tablespoons finely chopped
   mint
salt and pepper
crème fraîche (optional),
   to serve

....

Serves **4**
Prep time **10 minutes**
Cooking time **20 minutes**

....

1 Melt the butter in a saucepan, add the onion and potato, and cook for 5 minutes. Pour in the stock and bring to a boil, then reduce the heat and simmer gently for 10 minutes, or until the potato is tender. Add the peas to the pan and cook for another 3-4 minutes.

2 Season well with salt and pepper, then remove from the heat and stir in the mint. Blend the soup using a handheld blender. Ladle into serving bowls and top each portion with a dollop of crème fraîche, if desired.

VARIATION
For a chunky pea and ham soup, cook 1 chopped carrot and 1 chopped turnip with the onion and potato, then add 4 cups chicken stock. Once the root vegetables are tender, add 10 oz chopped ready-cooked ham, 4 finely chopped scallions, and 2 tablespoons chopped parsley with the peas and cook for 3-4 minutes. Do not blend the soup, but ladle into serving bowls and serve with crusty bread.

AFFORDABILITY
1

QUINOA &
tomato soup

1 Heat the oil in a saucepan. Add about a third of the kale and fry quickly, stirring continuously, until the kale starts to crisp. Lift out onto a plate with a slotted spoon.

2 Add the onion to the pan and fry for 4-5 minutes until softened. Add the stock and quinoa and bring to a gentle simmer. Cook for about 15 minutes, stirring frequently, until the quinoa is tender.

3 Add the tomatoes, tomato paste, sugar, oregano or thyme, and paprika and cook for about 10 minutes until the soup has thickened.

4 Stir in the uncooked kale and cook for another 5 minutes. Season with pepper. Ladle the soup into serving bowls and serve topped with the fried kale.

COOKING TIP
You'll find onions in many of the recipes in this book. If you want to chop them without ending up with red, watery eyes, try one of these tricks: chill them before chopping; chop them in a bowl of cold water; make sure your knife is super-sharp for less exposure of cut areas; wear a swim mask when cutting them.

1 tablespoon vegetable or mild olive oil
2 oz kale, tough stalks removed, and shredded
1 onion, chopped
generous 2 cups vegan stock
¼ cup quinoa, rinsed
13 oz can chopped tomatoes
1 tablespoon tomato paste
2 teaspoons brown sugar
1 teaspoon dried oregano or thyme
½ teaspoon paprika
pepper

Serves **2**
Prep time **10 minutes**
Cooking time **35 minutes**

CHORIZO &
BLACK BEAN SOUP

2 tablespoons vegetable oil
1 onion, finely chopped
4 oz chorizo sausage, finely
diced
1 red bell pepper, cored, seeded,
and chopped
1 garlic clove, chopped
1 teaspoon ground cumin
6⅓ cups hot chicken stock (see
page 11 for homemade)
2 x 13 oz cans black beans,
rinsed and drained
salt and pepper

To serve
2 tablespoons lime juice
4 tablespoons sour cream
handful of chopped cilantro
1 red chile, chopped

Serves **4**
Prep time **15 minutes**
Cooking time **20 minutes**

1 Heat the oil in a large heavy saucepan. Add the onion,
chorizo, red bell pepper, and garlic and cook for
7–10 minutes until softened, then stir in the cumin.
Pour in the stock and beans and simmer for 5–8 minutes.

2 Season to taste with salt and pepper, then use a potato
masher to coarsely mash some of the beans to thicken
the soup. Ladle the soup into serving bowls and sprinkle
a little lime juice over each portion. Add a spoonful of sour
cream, top with a sprinkling of the chopped cilantro and
chile, and serve immediately.

VARIATION
For a chorizo and black bean salad, rinse and drain a 13 oz
can black beans. Put the beans in a bowl and mix with
2 tablespoons extra virgin olive oil and a good squeeze of lime
juice. Season to taste with salt and pepper. Add 2 chopped
tomatoes, 2 chopped
scallions, and
a good handful of
chopped cilantro and
toss to combine.
Spoon the salad onto
a serving plate and
arrange slices of
fried chorizo sausage
on top. Serve with
crusty bread.

WINTERY
MINESTRONE
WITH PASTA
& BEANS

1. Heat the oil in a large heavy saucepan. Add the onion, celery, and carrot and cook for 5 minutes, or until softened, then add the garlic and cook for another 1 minute.

2. Pour in the tomatoes and stock, add the rosemary, and bring to a boil. Reduce the heat and simmer for 15 minutes.

3. Add the pasta and cabbage and cook for 5-7 minutes, or according to the package directions. Stir in the beans and heat through, then season to taste with salt and pepper. Ladle the soup into serving bowls, drizzle with the pesto, sprinkle with the grated Parmesan, and serve with crusty bread.

VARIATION

For a pasta and bean salad, cook 1½ cups orzo pasta in a large saucepan of lightly salted boiling water for 5 minutes. Drain, cool under cold running water, and drain again. Return the drained pasta to the pan. Toss with 1⅓ cups canned cannellini beans, rinsed and drained, ¾ cup halved cherry tomatoes, and 4 oz arugula. Stir in 4 tablespoons extra virgin olive oil and 1 tablespoon white wine vinegar, season to taste with salt and pepper, and serve sprinkled with grated Parmesan.

2 tablespoons olive oil
1 onion, chopped
1 celery stalk, chopped
1 carrot, chopped
1 garlic clove, crushed
13 oz can chopped tomatoes
6⅓ cups vegetable stock (see page 15 for homemade)
sprig of rosemary
¾ cup small soup pasta
3 oz Tuscan kale or other cabbage
1⅓ cups canned cannellini beans, rinsed and drained
4 tablespoons store-bought fresh green pesto
⅓ cup grated Parmesan cheese
salt and pepper
crusty bread, to serve

Serves **4**
Prep time **15 minutes**
Cooking time **30 minutes**

BALSAMIC ROAST VEG SALAD

Vegan

1 red onion, coarsely chopped
4 carrots, coarsely chopped
1 red bell pepper, cored, seeded, and cut into large pieces
1 sweet potato, peeled and cut into even-size pieces
13 oz zucchini, peeled and cut into even-size pieces
1 butternut squash, about 2 lb, peeled, seeded, and cut into chunks
2 tablespoons olive oil, plus extra to drizzle
$2/3$ cup balsamic vinegar
1 tablespoon chopped thyme
1 tablespoon chopped rosemary
3 oz arugula
salt and pepper

Serves **4**
Prep time **20 minutes**
Cooking time **30 minutes**

1 Put all the vegetables in a roasting pan, drizzle over the oil and balsamic vinegar and sprinkle with the herbs. Toss to make sure everything is well coated in the oil, then season to taste with salt and pepper. Roast in a preheated oven, 375°F, for 30 minutes, or until they are cooked and slightly crispy.

2 Remove the vegetables from the oven, let cool slightly, then toss with the arugula. Drizzle with olive oil, check the seasoning, and serve.

AFFORDABILITY 1

Greek salad
WITH TOASTED PITA

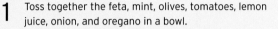

generous ¾ cup feta cheese,
  crumbled into smallish
  chunks
8–10 mint leaves, shredded
1 cup kalamata olives, pitted
2 tomatoes, chopped
juice of 1 large lemon
1 small red onion, thinly sliced
1 teaspoon dried oregano
4 pita breads
lemon wedges, to serve

Serves **4**
Prep time **15 minutes**
Cooking time **5 minutes**

1 Toss together the feta, mint, olives, tomatoes, lemon juice, onion, and oregano in a bowl.

2 Toast the pitas under a preheated hot broiler until lightly golden, then split open and toast the open sides.

3 Tear the hot pitas into bite-size pieces, then toss with the other salad ingredients in the bowl. Serve with lemon wedges.

AFFORDABILITY
1

FENNEL, ORANGE & olive salad

Vegan

1 large fennel bulb, about 11 oz, thinly sliced
8-10 black olives, pitted
1 tablespoon extra virgin olive oil
2 tablespoons lemon juice
2 oranges
salt and pepper

Serves **4-6**
Prep time **10 minutes**

1 Toss the fennel with the olives, oil, and lemon juice in a bowl. Season with salt and pepper.

2 Working over the salad bowl to catch the juice and, using a serrated knife, cut away the skin and pith of the oranges and slice thinly into circles. Add the orange slices to the fennel salad and toss very gently to combine.

AFFORDABILITY
1

CAULI CHEESE & LEEKS

1   Place the cauliflower and leek in a shallow ovenproof casserole and pour in the stock. Cover and simmer for 5 minutes, then pour away half the stock.

2   Blend the cornstarch with 3 tablespoons of the remaining stock in a mug, then stir in the crème fraîche. Pour the cornstarch mixture into the casserole, add half the cheddar, and cook for 1 minute. Season to taste with salt and pepper.

3   Sprinkle the remaining cheddar over the vegetables and place in a preheated oven, 400°F, for 15-20 minutes until golden and bubbling. Serve with crusty bread.

1 cauliflower, cut into florets
1 large leek, trimmed, cleaned, and sliced
generous 2 cups hot vegetable stock (see page 15 for homemade)
2 tablespoons cornstarch
2/3 cup crème fraîche
generous 1 cup grated cheddar cheese
salt and pepper
crusty bread, to serve

Serves **4**
Prep time **10 minutes**
Cooking time **30 minutes**

Eat-&-run SPINACH & CHICKPEA PITAS

V

AFFORDABILITY 1

1 Heat the oil in a skillet, add the onion, and fry, stirring, for 3-4 minutes until softened. Add the curry paste, tomato paste, honey, and the measured water and stir to mix. Add the chickpeas and cook for 5 minutes, or until hot and bubbling. Most of the water should have evaporated and the juices thickened.

2 Lightly toast the pita breads while you stir the spinach into the chickpeas until just wilted. Season to taste with salt and pepper.

3 Split the pita breads and spoon in the filling. Top with a little yogurt and serve.

1 tablespoon vegetable oil
1 small onion, sliced
1 teaspoon medium curry paste
1 tablespoon tomato paste
1 teaspoon honey
scant ½ cup water
1½ cups canned chickpeas, rinsed and drained
2 pita breads
1½ cups baby spinach leaves
2 tablespoons Greek yogurt
salt and pepper

Serves **2**
Prep time **10 minutes**
Cooking time **10 minutes**

MELTED CHEESE
& chicken
TORTILLA WEDGES

AFFORDABILITY 2

1 Lay 4 tortillas on 2 large baking sheets and sprinkle with the chicken, red bell peppers, and chile. Divide the chorizo and cheeses between the tortillas and sprinkle over the cilantro. Season to taste with salt and pepper.

2 Place another tortilla on top of each to make a sandwich, then gently press down with your hand. Place in a preheated oven, 375°F, and cook for 7 minutes, or until lightly crisp and the cheese has melted. Cut into wedges and serve with guacamole.

8 corn or wheat tortillas
2 ready-cooked chicken breasts, torn into shreds
2 ready-roasted red bell peppers, torn into strips
1 red chile, finely chopped
3½ oz chorizo sausage, thinly sliced
7 oz mozzarella cheese, thinly sliced
½ cup grated sharp cheddar cheese
handful of chopped cilantro
salt and pepper
ready-made guacamole, to serve

Serves **4**
Prep time **15 minutes**
Cooking time **10 minutes**

CHICKEN, OLIVE & CUMIN
COUSCOUS

1 Heat the oil in a saucepan, add the lemon, and cook over gentle heat for about 2 minutes until the lemon is soft. Stir in the honey, cumin, and garlic and heat through. Stir in the couscous, stock, chickpeas, olives, and chicken.

2 Remove from the heat and let stand for 5 minutes, or until the couscous is tender. Fluff up the couscous with a fork and stir in the cilantro and mint. Season to taste with salt and pepper and serve immediately.

VARIATION

For cumin-dusted chicken breasts with spicy olive couscous, heat 2 tablespoons oil in a skillet. Dust 4 small chicken breast fillets with 1 teaspoon ground cumin, season with salt and pepper, and cook for 5 minutes on each side, or until just cooked through. Stir in 1 crushed garlic clove and 2 teaspoons harissa or chili paste. Add 1½ cups couscous, 1¼ cups hot chicken stock, and ½ cup pitted green olives. Cover and let stand for 5 minutes, or until the couscous is tender. Fluff up the couscous with a fork and stir in a handful each of chopped mint and cilantro and the grated zest and juice of ½ lemon.

4 tablespoons olive oil
rind and flesh of ½ lemon, finely chopped
1 tablespoon honey
½ teaspoon ground cumin
1 garlic clove, crushed
1¾ cups couscous
1¼ cups hot chicken stock (see page 11 for homemade)
13 oz can chickpeas, rinsed and drained
½ cup green olives, pitted
2 ready-cooked chicken breasts, sliced
handful each of chopped cilantro and mint
salt and pepper

Serves **4**
Prep time **10 minutes, plus standing**
Cooking time **5 minutes**

CHICKEN, LENTILS & KALE

1. Heat half the oil in a large skillet with a lid. Add the chicken, season to taste with salt and pepper, and cook for 5 minutes, then turn over and cook for another 2 minutes, or until golden all over.

2. Add the remaining oil to the pan along with the garlic, kale, and a splash of water. Cover and cook for 7 minutes, or until the kale is tender and the chicken cooked through.

3. Stir in the lentils and heat through, then add the lemon juice and tomatoes. Taste and adjust the seasoning if necessary.

4. Lift the chicken breasts from the pan with a slotted spoon and transfer to a plate. Cut the chicken into thick slices and arrange on serving plates with the lentils and kale. Sprinkle over the goat cheese and serve immediately.

2 tablespoons olive oil
4 skinless chicken breast fillets
1 garlic clove, sliced
3½ oz kale, tough stalks removed, and chopped
8 oz can Puy lentils, rinsed and drained
2 tablespoons lemon juice
3 oz sunblush tomatoes
⅓ cup crumbled soft goat cheese
salt and pepper

Serves **4**
Prep time **10 minutes**
Cooking time **15 minutes**

AFFORDABILITY
2

CHICKEN
pad Thai

3 tablespoons vegetable oil
1 egg, lightly beaten
1 garlic clove, crushed
2 teaspoons finely grated fresh
    ginger root
2 scallions, sliced
10 oz ready-cooked rice
    noodles
1 cup bean sprouts
2 ready-cooked chicken
    breasts, torn into thin strips
2 tablespoons Thai fish sauce
2 teaspoons tamarind paste
2 teaspoons superfine sugar
pinch of chili powder

To garnish
scant ¼ cup ready-roasted
    peanuts, coarsely chopped
handful of chopped cilantro

Serves **4**
Prep time **10 minutes**
Cooking time **10 minutes**

1 Heat a large wok until smoking hot. Add 1 tablespoon of the oil and swirl around the pan, then pour in the egg. Stir around the pan and cook for 1–2 minutes until just cooked through. Lift the egg from the wok with a slotted spoon and transfer to a plate.

2 Heat the remaining oil in the wok, add the garlic, ginger, and scallions, and cook for 2 minutes, or until softened. Add the noodles, bean sprouts, and chicken to the wok. Stir in the fish sauce, tamarind paste, sugar, and chili powder and continue to cook, adding a splash of boiling water if necessary, until heated through.

3 Return the egg to the pan and mix in. Divide among serving bowls and garnish with the chopped peanuts and cilantro.

VARIATION
For a chicken noodle soup, put 3 cups chicken stock in a saucepan with 3 tablespoons rice wine, 2 tablespoons light soy sauce, and 1 star anise and simmer for 10 minutes. Mix 1⅓ cups ground chicken with 1 teaspoon grated fresh ginger root and 1 teaspoon soy sauce in a bowl. Shape the chicken mixture into balls and cook in the soup for 7 minutes. Stir in 3½ oz shiitake mushrooms and cook for another 3 minutes. Add 2 bok choy, quartered, and cook for 1 minute. Add 7 oz ready-cooked rice noodles and cook until heated through.

RÖSTI *with* SMOKED SALMON & ARUGULA SALAD

1 Place the potatoes and onion in a clean dish towel and squeeze to remove excess moisture. Season well with salt and pepper.

2 Heat the butter and 1 tablespoon of the oil in a nonstick skillet. Tip in the potato mixture and spread out to make an even layer, then cook for about 10 minutes, or until the underside is golden. Invert the rösti onto a plate, then carefully slide it back into the pan to cook the other side. Cook for another 5-8 minutes until cooked through and golden all over.

3 Meanwhile, make the salad. Mix the lemon juice with the remaining oil in a bowl and toss with the arugula.

4 Cut the rösti into wedges and serve with the arugula salad, slices of smoked salmon, and lemon wedges.

VARIATION

For a smoked salmon and arugula pasta, cook 1 lb fresh penne in a large saucepan of lightly salted boiling water according to the package directions. Drain and return to the pan. Add 4 tablespoons crème fraîche, 2 tablespoons lemon juice, and 6 oz smoked salmon, cut into strips. Toss through 3 oz arugula and season to taste with salt and pepper just before serving.

1½ lb waxy potatoes, coarsely grated
1 small onion, coarsely grated
3½ tablespoons butter
3 tablespoons olive oil
2 tablespoons lemon juice
3½ oz arugula
salt and pepper

To serve
8 oz smoked salmon
lemon wedges

Serves **4**
Prep time **10 minutes**
Cooking time **20 minutes**

Zingy SHRIMP WRAPS

AFFORDABILITY
2

1 Prepare the rice wrappers according to the package directions.

2 Toss together all the remaining ingredients in a bowl. Divide the mixture evenly among the wrappers and roll up, ensuring the ends are tucked in. Serve straight away.

12 rice wrappers
5 oz ready-cooked peeled shrimp, shredded
1 carrot, peeled and cut into very fine matchsticks
¼ cucumber, cut into very fine matchsticks
1 small bunch of cilantro, chopped
8 mint leaves, chopped
½ mango, peeled and cut into small strips
1 teaspoon sesame oil
1 teaspoon lime juice
handful of peanuts, coarsely chopped (optional)
½ red chile, seeded and finely chopped (optional)

Makes **12**
Prep time **15 minutes**

STUDENT TIP

Even if you lack outdoor space you can still grow your own salad greens and herbs—a few pots on the windowsill is all you need for a collection of fresh ingredients that will liven up pasta sauces, casseroles, and salads for the price of a few packages of seeds.

Caramelized
PARSNIPS

1¼ lb parsnips, scrubbed or peeled
3½ tablespoons butter
¾ cup diced bacon
3 tablespoons superfine sugar
⅓ cup pine nuts
5 tablespoons chopped thyme

Serves **2**
Prep time **5 minutes**
Cooking time **20 minutes**

1 Cut the parsnips in half widthwise, then cut the chunky tops into quarters lengthwise and the slim bottom halves in half lengthwise.

2 Heat the butter in a large skillet, add the bacon and parsnips, and cook over medium heat for about 15 minutes, turning and tossing occasionally, until the parsnips are golden and softened and the bacon is crisp.

3 Add the sugar and pine nuts and cook for another 2-3 minutes until lightly caramelized. Toss with the thyme and serve.

VARIATION

For a bacon, pine nut, and parsnip rösti, grate 11½ oz peeled parsnips into a bowl and mix with 2 oz ready-cooked bacon slices, snipped into small pieces, and 2 tablespoons chopped parsley. Divide the mixture and squeeze together to form 4 balls, then flatten into patties. Heat 3½ tablespoons butter in a large skillet, add the patties, and cook over high heat for 2 minutes on each side, or until golden. Serve hot with a green salad and sprinkled with pine nuts.

AFFORDABILITY
1

SPICY MUSHROOMS & CAULI

(V)

2 tablespoons sunflower oil
8 scallions, cut into 2 inch
   lengths
2 teaspoons grated garlic
2 teaspoons ground ginger
2 tablespoons hot curry
   powder
7 oz baby button mushrooms
10 oz cauliflower florets
2 red bell peppers, cored,
   seeded, and cut into chunks
13 oz can chopped tomatoes
scant 1½ cups canned
   chickpeas, rinsed and drained
salt and pepper
large handful of chopped mint,
   to garnish
warm naan breads, to serve

Serves **4**
Prep time **10 minutes**
Cooking time **25 minutes**

1 Heat the oil in a large skillet, add the scallions, and fry over medium heat for 1-2 minutes. Add the garlic, ginger, and curry powder and fry, stirring, for 20-30 seconds until fragrant, then stir in the mushrooms, cauliflower, and red bell peppers and fry for another 2-3 minutes.

2 Stir in the tomatoes and bring to a boil. Reduce the heat to medium and simmer for 10-15 minutes, stirring occasionally. Add the chickpeas, season with salt and pepper, and bring back to a boil. Garnish with the chopped mint and serve with warm naan breads.

VARIATION

For a spicy mushroom, cauliflower, and chickpea rice, heat 2 tablespoons sunflower oil in a large skillet until hot, add 1 chopped onion, 1 seeded and chopped red chile, 3½ oz baby button mushrooms, 1 tablespoon curry powder, 3½ oz small cauliflower florets, ¾ cup canned chickpeas, rinsed and drained, 1 teaspoon ginger paste, and 1 teaspoon garlic paste, and stir-fry over high heat for 6-8 minutes. Add 3½ cups ready-cooked basmati or long-grain rice and stir-fry for another 3-4 minutes until piping hot. Season with salt and pepper, then serve immediately.

AFFORDABILITY **1**

flash-in-the-pan RATATOUILLE

Vegan

scant ½ cup olive oil
2 onions, chopped
1 eggplant, cut into ¾ inch cubes
2 large zucchini, cut into ¾ inch cubes
1 red bell pepper, cored, seeded, and cut into ¾ inch pieces
1 yellow bell pepper, cored, seeded, and cut into ¾ inch pieces
2 garlic cloves, crushed
13 oz can chopped tomatoes
2-3 tablespoons balsamic vinegar
1 teaspoon soft brown sugar
salt and pepper

To garnish
10-12 black olives, pitted
torn basil leaves

Serves **4**
Prep time **15 minutes**
Cooking time **20 minutes**

1 Heat the oil in a large saucepan until very hot. Add all of the vegetables, except the tomatoes, and stir-fry for a few minutes.

2 Add the tomatoes, balsamic vinegar, and sugar, season with salt and pepper, and stir well. Cover tightly and simmer for 15 minutes, or until the vegetables are cooked.

3 Remove from the heat, sprinkle over the olives and torn basil leaves, and serve.

VARIATION
For a Mediterranean-style thick vegetable soup, follow the recipe above, then add 1¼ cups hot vegetable stock to the cooked ratatouille and use a handheld blender to blend until fairly smooth. Ladle the soup into serving bowls and garnish with basil leaves.

AFFORDABILITY 1

MOLASSES & MUSTARD BEANS

1. Put all the ingredients into an ovenproof casserole and bring slowly to a boil, stirring occasionally.

2. Cover, transfer to a preheated oven, 325°F, and bake for 1 hour. Remove the lid and bake for another 30 minutes. Serve with garlic-rubbed bread.

ACCOMPANIMENT TIP

For a garlic-rubbed bread, to serve as an accompaniment, heat a griddle pan until hot, add 6 thick slices of sourdough bread, and cook for 2 minutes on each side until lightly charred. Rub each bread slice with a peeled garlic clove (or 2) and drizzle with extra virgin olive oil.

1 carrot, diced
1 celery stalk, chopped
1 onion, chopped
2 garlic cloves, crushed
2 x 13 oz cans soybeans, drained
2¾ cups strained tomatoes
3 oz smoked bacon slices, diced
2 tablespoons molasses
2 teaspoons Dijon mustard
salt and pepper
Garlic-Rubbed Bread (see tip), to serve

Serves **6**
Prep time **10 minutes**
Cooking time **1 hour 35 minutes**

AFFORDABILITY

1

SPICED CORN
WITH AVOCADO & TOMATO

V

2 corn cobs
3 tablespoons sunflower oil
1 red bell pepper, halved
  lengthwise, cored, and
  seeded
1 ripe avocado
½ Scotch bonnet chile or hot
  red chile, seeded and finely
  chopped
6 plum tomatoes, coarsely
  chopped
1 small bunch of cilantro, leaves
  coarsely chopped
juice of 2 limes
⅔ cup extra virgin olive oil
salt and pepper
warm flatbreads, to serve

Serves **4**
Prep time **20 minutes, plus
  cooling**
Cooking time **20 minutes**

1 Blanch the corn cobs in a large saucepan of boiling
  water for 30-45 seconds. Drain, then brush the cobs
  with sunflower oil and cook under a broiler preheated
  to its highest setting for 4-5 minutes, turning frequently,
  until beginning to char at the edges. Using a sharp knife,
  cut the kernels from the cobs and put in a large bowl.

2 Cook the red bell pepper halves, skin side up, under the
  preheated broiler for 6-8 minutes until the skin begins
  to blister. Place in a plastic food bag, seal, and leave for
  5 minutes. When cool, peel away the blackened skin,
  then dice the flesh and add to the bowl of corn.

3 Halve, peel, and pit the avocado, then dice the flesh.
  Stir into the corn mixture with the chile and tomatoes.

4 Make the dressing. Mix together the cilantro, lime juice,
  and olive oil in a mug, then season with salt and pepper
  and whisk well.

5 Pour the dressing over the corn mixture and toss
  through gently. Serve with warm flatbreads.

AFFORDABILITY
1

Stir-fried veg RICE

Vegan

2 tablespoons sunflower oil
6 scallions, cut diagonally into
  1 inch lengths
2 garlic cloves, crushed
1 teaspoon finely grated fresh
  ginger root
1 red bell pepper, cored, seeded,
  and finely chopped
1 carrot, peeled and finely diced
2 cups peas
3½ cups ready-cooked
  long-grain rice
1 tablespoon dark soy sauce
1 tablespoon sweet chili sauce
chopped cilantro and mint, to
  garnish

Serves **4**
Prep time **10 minutes**
Cooking time **15 minutes**

1 Heat the oil in a large nonstick wok. Add the scallions, garlic, and ginger and stir-fry over high heat for 4-5 minutes, then add the red bell pepper, carrot, and peas and stir-fry for 3-4 minutes.

2 Stir in the rice and soy and sweet chili sauces and stir-fry for 3-4 minutes until the rice is heated through and piping hot. Remove from the heat and serve immediately, garnished with the chopped herbs.

AFFORDABILITY
1

SPINACH & POTATO
TORTILLA Ⓥ

3 tablespoons olive oil
2 onions, finely chopped
8 oz ready-cooked potatoes, peeled and cut into ½ inch cubes
2 garlic cloves, finely chopped
7 oz ready-cooked spinach, drained thoroughly, and coarsely chopped
4 tablespoons finely chopped ready-roasted red bell pepper
5 eggs, lightly beaten
3-4 tablespoons grated Manchego cheese
salt and pepper

Serves **4**
Prep time **15 minutes**
Cooking time **20 minutes**

1 Heat the oil in an ovenproof, nonstick skillet. Add the onions and potatoes and cook gently over medium heat for 3-4 minutes, turning and stirring often, until the vegetables have softened but not colored. Stir in the garlic, spinach, and red pepper.

2 Season the eggs with salt and pepper, then pour them into the skillet, shaking the pan so that the egg is evenly spread. Cook gently for 8-10 minutes until the tortilla is set at the bottom.

3 Sprinkle over the cheese. Place the skillet under a preheated medium-hot broiler and cook for 3-4 minutes until the top is set and golden.

4 Cut the tortilla into bite-size squares or triangles and serve warm or at room temperature.

VARIATION

For a spinach and potato sauté, heat 1 tablespoon vegetable oil in a large skillet. Add 2 chopped garlic cloves, 1 finely chopped onion, and 1 tablespoon curry powder. Stir in scant ½ cup strained tomatoes, 6 cups baby spinach leaves, and 7 oz ready-cooked potatoes, cubed. Sauté over high heat for 2-3 minutes until piping hot. Season with salt and pepper and serve with crusty bread or boiled rice.

TORTILLA (V)
with tomato & arugula salad

1 Heat the olive oil in an ovenproof nonstick skillet. Add the onion and potato and cook for 5-10 minutes until golden, then pour in the measured water. Simmer gently until the potatoes are very tender, then carefully pour away any excess liquid.

2 Season the eggs with salt and pepper, then pour them into the pan and stir gently. Cook over low heat for 10-15 minutes until set all the way through, finishing off under a preheated broiler to set the top if necessary.

3 To make the salad, toss the arugula with the extra virgin olive oil, lemon juice, and tomatoes in a bowl. Season well with salt and pepper and add the Parmesan shavings.

4 To serve, cut the tortilla into wedges and serve topped with the salad.

VARIATION
For egg, tomato, and arugula wraps, crack 4 eggs into a lightly greased nonstick skillet. Dot with scant ¼ cup mascarpone cheese and season well with salt and pepper. Cook over low heat for 2-3 minutes until starting to set. Stir in 1 chopped tomato and cook for another 1 minute, or until just set. Spoon over 4 wheat tortilla wraps, then sprinkle with 2 oz arugula and a little crumbled goat cheese. Wrap up the tortillas and serve.

4 tablespoons olive oil
1 onion, finely chopped
3 potatoes, thickly sliced
scant 1 cup water
5 eggs, beaten

Tomato & arugula salad
3 oz arugula
2 tablespoons extra virgin olive oil
2 tablespoons lemon juice
2 oz sunblush tomatoes
handful of Parmesan cheese shavings
salt and pepper

Serves **4**
Prep time **10 minutes**
Cooking time **20-30 minutes**

AFFORDABILITY 1

PAN-COOKED *eggs*  Ⓥ

2 tablespoons butter
1 leek, trimmed, cleaned, and
    thinly sliced
½ teaspoon dried red pepper
    flakes
5 cups baby spinach leaves
2 eggs
3 tablespoons plain yogurt
pinch of paprika
salt and pepper

Serves **2**
Prep time **5 minutes**
Cooking time **10 minutes**

1 Heat the butter in a skillet, add the leek and red pepper flakes, and cook over medium-high heat for 4–5 minutes until softened. Add the spinach and season well with salt and pepper, then toss and cook for 2 minutes until the spinach has wilted.

2 Make 2 hollows in the vegetables and break an egg into each hollow. Cook over low heat for 2–3 minutes until the eggs are set. Spoon the yogurt on top and sprinkle with the paprika.

AFFORDABILITY 1

STUDENT TIP

Don't rely on corner stores and convenience stores for your groceries. Plan in advance and shop at larger grocery stores and food markets —your shopping will be much cheaper.

PIZZA FIORENTINA Ⓥ

2½ cups baby spinach leaves
4 large wheat tortillas
   or flatbreads
²⁄₃ cup ready-made tomato
   sauce
4 oz mozzarella cheese, sliced
4 eggs
⅓ cup grated Parmesan cheese

Serves **4**
Prep time **10 minutes**
Cooking time **10 minutes**

1 Place the spinach in a strainer and pour over boiling water until it has wilted, then squeeze thoroughly to remove excess water.

2 Arrange the tortillas on 4 pizza trays. Spoon the tomato sauce over the tortillas, then sprinkle over the spinach and arrange the mozzarella on top. Crack an egg in the center of each pizza.

3 Sprinkle the Parmesan over the pizzas, then place in a preheated oven, 425°F, for 5-7 minutes until the egg whites are just set.

AFFORDABILITY
1

PECORINO & CHILE
Omelet

1 tablespoon butter
1 egg, lightly beaten
⅓ cup grated pecorino cheese
pinch of dried red pepper
  flakes
green salad, to serve

Serves **1**
Prep time **5 minutes**
Cooking time **10 minutes**

1 Heat the butter in a small skillet until foaming. Pour in the egg and stir around the pan, then let cook for 30 seconds until starting to set. Sprinkle over the pecorino and red pepper flakes and cook until the omelet is set. Roll up the omelet and serve with a green salad.

STUDENT TIP
Local farmers' markets overflow with great-value seasonal produce and this is the time to really put your freezer to work: wash and bag up seasonal berries; peel and chop apples and pears; and peel and dice vegetables—ready to prepare casseroles, compotes, and soups.

Cheesy TURKEY & CRANBERRY MELTS

1 Split the rolls in half and spread the base of each one with the mustard and the top halves of each one with the cranberry sauce. Arrange the turkey slices and cheese on top of the mustard and sandwich the rolls together.

2 Heat a dry skillet until hot, add the sandwiches, and cook over medium-high heat for 4 minutes on each side, or until golden and the cheese has melted. Serve hot.

VARIATION

For avocado, blue cheese and spinach melts, split the rolls in half and spread the base of each one with a little butter. Mash together 1 peeled, pitted, and sliced avocado, scant ½ cup crumbled blue cheese, and 2 tablespoons thick cream in a bowl. Divide the avocado mixture between the roll bases, add a few baby spinach leaves and then add the roll tops. Cook as above until the filling starts to ooze.

4 flat rolls
2 tablespoons whole-grain mustard
2 tablespoons cranberry sauce
7 oz ready-cooked turkey breast, sliced
generous 1⅓ cups grated Cheddar cheese

Serves **4**
Prep time **5 minutes**
Cooking time **10 minutes**

Egg pots
WITH SMOKED SALMON

butter, for greasing
7 oz smoked salmon trimmings
2 tablespoons chopped chives
4 eggs
4 tablespoons heavy cream
pepper
toasted bread, to serve

Serves **4**
Prep time **5 minutes**
Cooking time **10–15 minutes**

1 Grease 4 ramekins with butter. Divide the smoked salmon and chives among the prepared ramekins. Using the back of a spoon, make a small hollow in the top of the salmon in each ramekin. Break an egg into each hollow, sprinkle with a little pepper, and spoon the cream over the top.

2 Put the ramekins in a roasting pan and half-fill the pan with boiling water. Bake in a preheated oven, 350°F, for 10–15 minutes until the eggs have just set.

3 Remove from the oven and let cool for a few minutes, then serve with the toasted bread.

ACCOMPANIMENT TIP
For a homemade Melba toast, to serve as an accompaniment, toast 4 slices of bread lightly on both sides. While hot, trim off the crusts, then split the toast in half widthwise. Lay the toast, cut side up, on a baking sheet and bake in the bottom of the oven until dry.

AFFORDABILITY
2

ZUCCHINI & RICOTTA BAKES

1   Lightly grease 8 holes in a large muffin pan with butter.
    Use a vegetable peeler to make 16 long ribbons of
    zucchini and set aside. Coarsely grate the remainder
    of the zucchini onto a clean dish towel and squeeze
    to remove excess moisture.

2   To make the filling, mix the grated zucchini with the
    remaining ingredients in a bowl and season well with
    salt and pepper.

3   Arrange 2 zucchini ribbons in a cross shape in each
    hole of the prepared muffin pan. Spoon in the filling and
    fold over the overhanging zucchini ends. Place in a
    preheated oven, 375°F, for 15–20 minutes until golden
    and cooked through. Turn out onto serving plates.

VARIATION

For penne with zucchini and ricotta, cook 1 lb fresh penne
pasta in a large saucepan of lightly salted boiling water
according to the package directions, adding ⅔ cup frozen
peas for the last 2 minutes of cooking time. Drain and
return the pasta and peas to the pan. Add the finely
grated zest of 1 lemon and 2 tablespoons lemon juice.
Use a vegetable peeler to slice 2 zucchini into long
ribbons. Add the zucchini ribbons to the pan with 2 oz
arugula, 2 tablespoons olive oil, and ⅓ cup grated
Parmesan cheese. Season to taste with salt and pepper.
Divide among serving bowls and top with a spoonful
of ricotta cheese.

butter, for greasing
2 zucchini
1¾ cups fresh white bread
    crumbs
1 cup ricotta cheese
generous 1 cup grated
    Parmesan cheese
2 eggs, beaten
1 garlic clove, crushed
handful of chopped basil
salt and pepper

Serves **4**
Prep time **10 minutes**
Cooking time **15–20 minutes**

AFFORDABILITY

1

Stuffed ZUCCHINI

(V)

1 Slice the zucchini in half horizontally and then scoop out the middle of each one, setting aside the flesh. Place the zucchini halves, cut side up, in a roasting pan and bake in a preheated oven, 400°F, for 10 minutes.

2 Meanwhile, to make the filling, chop the reserved zucchini flesh and mix it in a bowl with the tomatoes, mozzarella, and basil. Season to taste with salt and pepper.

3 Remove the zucchini halves from the oven and spoon the filling into each one. Sprinkle with the Parmesan and return to the oven for 15 minutes, or until golden.

VARIATION
For griddled zucchini with mozzarella, use a vegetable peeler to thinly slice 4 zucchini lengthwise. Toss the zucchini in a bowl with 2 tablespoons olive oil and then cook them on a preheated hot griddle pan for 2-3 minutes on both sides, until griddle marks start to show. Served topped with 7 oz torn mozzarella cheese and 6-8 torn basil leaves. Drizzle with a little olive oil, a squeeze of lemon juice, and a grinding of pepper.

4 zucchini
6 oz plum tomatoes, chopped
1¾ cups grated mozzarella cheese
2 tablespoons shredded basil
⅓ cup grated Parmesan cheese
salt and pepper

Serves **4**
Prep time **10 minutes**
Cooking time **25 minutes**

feta-stuffed PEPPERS Ⓥ

1 tablespoon olive oil
4 long peppers
2 egg yolks
1¾ cups crumbled feta cheese
3 tablespoons plain yogurt
finely grated zest of ½ lemon
1 teaspoon chopped oregano

Serves **4**
Prep time **10 minutes, plus
    cooling**
Cooking time **10-15 minutes**

1 Rub the oil over the long peppers, arrange them in a broiler pan, and cook under a preheated hot broiler for 5 minutes, turning once, until just soft. Let cool for a couple of minutes, then cut in half lengthwise and remove the seeds.

2 Place the egg yolks, three-quarters of the feta, the yogurt, and lemon zest in a food processor and blend until smooth. (If you don't have a food processor, put the ingredients in a bowl, mash the feta with a fork, and then beat until smooth.) Spoon the mixture into the peppers, then crumble the remaining feta on top and sprinkle with the oregano.

3 Return the peppers to the broiler and cook for 5-7 minutes until golden and cooked through. Let set for a couple of minutes before serving.

VARIATION
For a feta and pepper salad, mash 3½ oz feta cheese with 2 tablespoons heavy cream in a bowl until well combined and smooth. Spoon the mixture over 4 ready-roasted pepper halves and roll up. Make a dressing by whisking 1 tablespoon lemon juice with 3 tablespoons olive oil and ½ teaspoon dried oregano in a separate bowl, then season to taste with salt and pepper. Toss the dressing together with 3½ oz corn salad, ½ sliced cucumber, and ½ cup pitted black olives. Arrange the salad on a serving platter, cut the peppers into thick slices, and arrange on top. Serve with crusty bread.

AFFORDABILITY
1

VEGETABLE BOLOGNESE

1 Heat the oil in a large heavy saucepan. Add the onion, garlic, celery, carrot, and mushrooms and cook over medium heat, stirring frequently, for 5 minutes, or until softened. Add the tomato paste and cook, stirring, for another 1 minute.

2 Pour in the tomatoes and wine or stock, then add the dried herbs, yeast extract, and vegetable protein. Bring to a boil, then reduce the heat, cover, and simmer for 30-40 minutes until the vegetable protein is tender.

3 Stir in the parsley and season well with salt and pepper. Divide the sauce between serving plates and serve immediately with cooked spaghetti and a sprinkling of grated Parmesan.

1 tablespoon vegetable oil
1 onion, finely chopped
1 garlic clove, finely chopped
1 celery stalk, finely chopped
1 carrot, finely chopped
3 oz cremini mushrooms, coarsely chopped
1 tablespoon tomato paste
13 oz can chopped tomatoes
1 cup red wine or vegetable stock (see page 15 for homemade)
pinch of dried mixed herbs
1 teaspoon yeast extract
5 oz textured vegetable protein (TVP)
2 tablespoons chopped parsley
salt and pepper

To serve
cooked spaghetti
grated Parmesan cheese

Serves **2**
Prep time **10 minutes**
Cooking time **40-50 minutes**

Baked MUSHROOMS
WITH GOAT CHEESE & ARUGULA

1 lb new potatoes, halved
3 tablespoons olive oil
7 oz portobello mushrooms
2 tablespoons chopped thyme
6 garlic cloves, unpeeled
scant ¼ cup soft goat cheese
¾ cup cherry tomatoes
salt and pepper
scant ¼ cup toasted pine nuts,
   to garnish
3 oz arugula, to serve

Serves **4**
Prep time **5 minutes**
Cooking time **25 minutes**

1 Put the potatoes in a large roasting pan, drizzle over 2 tablespoons olive oil, and toss to make sure the potatoes are well coated in oil. Bake in a preheated oven, 425°F, for 15 minutes, turning once halfway through the cooking time.

2 Add the mushrooms, stem side up, to the pan, sprinkle over the thyme and garlic, drizzle over the remaining oil, and season well with salt and pepper. Place a little goat cheese on top of each mushroom and return to the oven for another 5 minutes.

3 Add the cherry tomatoes to the pan and return to the oven for 5 minutes more, or until the potatoes and mushrooms are cooked through. Garnish with the pine nuts and serve with the arugula.

VARIATION
For mushroom burgers with goat cheese and arugula, place 4 large portobello mushrooms on a lightly greased baking sheet and season well. Bake in a preheated oven, 425°F, for 15 minutes, or until the mushrooms are tender. Split and lightly toast 4 ciabatta rolls. Place a mushroom on the bottom half of each roll, then divide scant ¼ cup soft goat cheese, 4 tablespoons store-bought fresh green pesto, and 1 thinly sliced tomato among them. Replace the tops of the rolls and serve the burgers with an arugula salad.

AFFORDABILITY
1

SPICY PANEER
WITH TOMATOES, PEAS & BEANS

1. Heat half the oil in a large skillet with a lid. Add the paneer, season well with salt and pepper, and cook for 3-4 minutes until golden all over. Lift out with a slotted spoon onto a plate.

2. Add the remaining oil and the onion to the pan and cook for 5 minutes until softened. Stir in the garlic and ginger and cook for another 1 minute, then add the spices and cook for 30 seconds.

3. Stir in the tomato paste and stock, then add the beans and return the paneer to the pan. Season to taste with salt and pepper, cover, and simmer for 5 minutes.

4. Add the peas and tomatoes and cook for another 3 minutes, then stir in the garam masala. Divide among serving bowls and serve with chapattis.

2 tablespoons vegetable oil
8 oz paneer, diced
1 onion, finely chopped
2 garlic cloves, chopped
2 teaspoons finely grated fresh ginger root
1 teaspoon ground coriander
1 teaspoon paprika
1 teaspoon tomato paste
1/2 cup hot vegetable stock (see page 15 for homemade)
5 oz green beans, trimmed
scant 1 1/2 cups frozen peas
3/4 cup chopped tomatoes
1 teaspoon garam masala
salt and pepper
chapattis, to serve

Serves **4**
Prep time **15 minutes**
Cooking time **20 minutes**

AFFORDABILITY 1

VEGETABLE & TOFU STIR-FRY

Vegan

1 Heat 1 tablespoon of the oil in a wok until starting to smoke, add the tofu, and stir-fry over high heat for 2 minutes, or until golden. Lift out with a slotted spoon onto a plate.

2 Heat the remaining oil in the wok, add the onion and carrots, and stir-fry for 1½ minutes. Add the broccoli and red bell pepper and stir-fry for 1 minute, then add the zucchini and snap peas and stir-fry for 1 minute.

3 Combine the soy and chili sauces and the measured water in a mug, pour into the wok, then return the tofu to the wok and cook for 1 minute. Divide among serving bowls and garnish with the chopped red chiles and basil leaves.

ACCOMPANIMENT TIP
For sesame noodles, to serve as an accompaniment, put 12 oz egg thread noodles in a large heatproof bowl, pour over enough boiling water to cover, and let stand for 4 minutes, or until just tender. Drain well, then toss with 1 tablespoon light soy sauce and 2 teaspoons sesame oil. Serve sprinkled with 1 tablespoon toasted sesame seeds.

3 tablespoons sunflower oil
10 oz firm tofu, cubed
1 onion, sliced
2 carrots, sliced
5 oz broccoli, broken into small florets and stalks sliced
1 red bell pepper, cored, seeded and sliced
1 large zucchini, sliced
5 oz sugar snap peas
2 tablespoons soy sauce
2 tablespoons sweet chili sauce
½ cup water

To garnish
chopped red chiles
Thai or ordinary basil leaves

Serves **4**
Prep time **10 minutes**
Cooking time **10 minutes**

AFFORDABILITY
1

Okra & Coconut STEW *Vegan*

1 Trim the stalk ends from the okra and cut the pods into ¾ inch lengths.

2 Heat 2 tablespoons of the oil in a large, deep-sided skillet with a lid or shallow ovenproof casserole and fry the okra for 5 minutes. Lift out with a slotted spoon onto a plate.

3 Add the remaining oil to the pan or casserole and very gently fry the onions, green bell peppers, and celery, stirring frequently, for 10 minutes, or until softened but not browned. Add the garlic, spice blend, and turmeric and cook for 1 minute.

4 Pour in the stock and coconut milk and bring to a boil. Reduce the heat, cover, and cook gently for 10 minutes. Return the okra to the pan with the corn, lime juice, and cilantro and cook for another 10 minutes. Season to taste with salt and pepper and serve.

ACCOMPANIMENT TIP

For an easy cornbread, to serve as an accompaniment, mix together 1 cup cornmeal, ¾ cup all-purpose flour, 1 teaspoon salt, 2 teaspoons baking powder, ½ teaspoon ground cumin, and ½ teaspoon dried red pepper flakes in a bowl. Beat 1 egg with scant 1 cup milk in a mug, pour into the cornmeal mixture, and mix gently until just combined (do not overmix). Turn into a greased 7½ x 3½ inch loaf pan. Bake in a preheated oven, 375°F, for 30 minutes, or until firm to the touch. Serve warm or transfer to a wire rack to cool.

12 oz okra
4 tablespoons vegetable oil
2 onions, chopped
2 green bell peppers, cored, seeded, and cut into chunks
3 celery stalks, thinly sliced
3 garlic cloves, crushed
4 teaspoons Cajun spice blend
½ teaspoon ground turmeric
1¼ cups vegetable stock (see page 15 for homemade)
14 oz can coconut milk
scant ½ cup frozen corn
juice of 1 lime
4 tablespoons chopped cilantro
salt and pepper

Serves **3-4**
Prep time **15 minutes**
Cooking time **40 minutes**

Spiced CHICKPEAS & KALE

Vegan

3 tablespoons vegetable oil
3 red onions, cut into wedges
2 tablespoons mild curry paste
13 oz can chopped tomatoes
13 oz can chickpeas, rinsed and
   drained
1¼ cups vegetable stock (see
   page 15 for homemade)
2 teaspoons soft light brown
   sugar
3½ oz kale, tough stalks
   removed
salt and pepper

Serves **4**
Prep time **10 minutes**
Cooking time **35 minutes**

1 Heat the oil in a large saucepan and fry the onions for 5 minutes, or until beginning to color. Stir in the curry paste and then the tomatoes, chickpeas, stock, and sugar. Bring to a boil, then reduce the heat, cover, and simmer gently for 20 minutes.

2 Stir in the kale and cook gently for another 10 minutes. Season to taste with salt and pepper and serve.

ACCOMPANIMENT TIP
For sesame flatbreads, to serve as an accompaniment, place 2 cups all-purpose flour, 1 teaspoon salt, and scant ¼ cup sesame seeds in a bowl. Add 3 tablespoons vegetable oil and ½ cup cold water and mix with a round-bladed knife to a dough, adding a dash more water if the dough feels dry. Divide into 8 pieces and very thinly roll out each piece on a lightly floured counter until about ⅛ inch thick. Heat a griddle or large dry skillet until hot and cook the flatbreads for about 2 minutes on each side until pale golden.

AFFORDABILITY
1

TOMATO & BASIL TART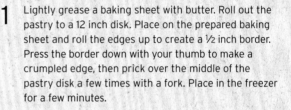

butter for greasing
12 oz ready-made puff pastry
all-purpose flour, for dusting
1 egg, beaten
scant 1 cup mascarpone cheese
¾ cup grated Parmesan
   cheese
handful of chopped basil, plus
   extra to garnish
scant 1 cup cherry tomatoes,
   halved
1 tablespoon olive oil
salt and pepper

Serves **4**
Prep time **15 minutes**
Cooking time **20-25 minutes**

1 Lightly grease a baking sheet with butter. Roll out the pastry to a 12 inch disk. Place on the prepared baking sheet and roll the edges up to create a ½ inch border. Press the border down with your thumb to make a crumpled edge, then prick over the middle of the pastry disk a few times with a fork. Place in the freezer for a few minutes.

2 Brush the border of the pastry with a little of the beaten egg. Mix together the mascarpone, remaining egg, Parmesan, and basil in a bowl, season to taste with salt and pepper, and spread over the center of the tart. Arrange the tomatoes on top of the tart and drizzle over the oil. Bake in a preheated oven, 425°F, for 20-25 minutes until golden and crisp.

AFFORDABILITY
1

MAD ABOUT MAINS

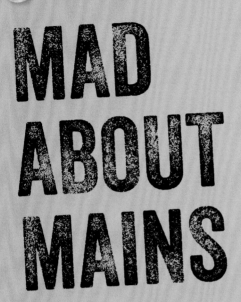

ROAST CHICKEN WITH BUTTERNUT SQUASH

PAELLA

CHICKEN WITH SPRING HERBS

BEEF & PICKLED ONION STEW

Salmon
WITH GREEN VEGETABLES

1 tablespoon olive oil
1 leek, trimmed, cleaned, and
    thinly sliced
generous 1 cup fish stock (see
    page 104 for homemade)
scant 1 cup crème fraîche
1 cup frozen peas
1 cup frozen soy- or fava beans
4 chunky skinless salmon fillets,
    about 5 oz each
2 tablespoons snipped chives
pepper
mashed potato, to serve

Serves **4**
Prep time **5 minutes**
Cooking time **20 minutes**

1 Heat the oil in a large heavy skillet with a lid and cook the leek over medium heat, stirring frequently, for 3 minutes, or until softened. Pour in the stock, bring to a boil, and continue boiling for 2 minutes, or until reduced a little.

2 Add the crème fraîche and stir well to mix. Add the peas, soy- or fava beans, and salmon and return to a boil. Reduce the heat, cover, and simmer for 10 minutes, or until the fish is opaque and cooked through and the peas and beans are piping hot.

3 Sprinkle over the chives, season with pepper, and serve spooned over instant mashed potato.

VARIATION
For creamy salmon and green vegetables, melt 1 tablespoon butter in a heavy skillet and cook 2 skinless salmon fillets, about 5 oz each, cut into small cubes, and scant ½ cup frozen peas over medium heat, stirring gently, for 3 minutes. Add 16 thin asparagus spears, trimmed and chopped into 1½ inch pieces, pour in 5 tablespoons fish stock and generous 1 cup light cream, and cook gently for another 5 minutes. Garnish with torn basil or parsley leaves and serve with cooked pasta.

AFFORDABILITY
3

CHICKEN, HAM & CABBAGE STEW

1 Drain the beans and transfer to a large saucepan. Cover with fresh cold water and bring to a boil. Reduce the heat and simmer for 40 minutes, or until just tender. Drain and set aside.

2 Add the drained ham to the empty bean pan with the chicken legs, onions, and bay leaves. Pour over the measured water and bring to a gentle simmer. Cover and cook very gently for 1 hour.

3 Cut the potatoes into small chunks and add to the pan with the beans and paprika. Cook very gently, covered, for another 20 minutes, or until the potatoes are tender.

4 Lift the chicken and ham from the pan with a slotted spoon and transfer to a plate. Once cool enough to handle, pull the meat from the bones, discarding the skin. Shred or chop all the meat into small pieces.

5 Return the meat to the pan. Stir in the cabbage and cilantro and heat through gently. Season with pepper and serve.

scant 1 cup dried haricot beans, soaked in a bowl of cold water overnight
1 ham hock or joint, about 1½ lb, soaked in a bowl of cold water overnight
4 chicken legs
2 onions, chopped
3 bay leaves
5 cups cold water
1 lb mealy potatoes
1 tablespoon paprika
3⅓ cups green cabbage, shredded
½ cup coarsely chopped cilantro
pepper

Serves **6**
Prep time **30 minutes, plus overnight soaking**
Cooking time **2 hours 10 minutes**

Lemon chili CHICKEN

1 chicken, about 3½ lb, jointed
8 garlic cloves, peeled
4 juicy lemons, quartered and
  squeezed, skins set aside
1 small red chile, seeded and
  chopped
2 tablespoons orange blossom
  honey
4 tablespoons chopped parsley,
  plus sprigs to garnish
salt and pepper

Serves **4**
Prep time **25 minutes, plus
  marinating**
Cooking time **45 minutes**

1 Arrange the chicken pieces in a shallow, ovenproof casserole. Crush 2 of the garlic cloves, then put them in a mug with the lemon juice, chile, and honey and stir well. Pour the mixture over the chicken. Tuck the lemon skins around the meat, cover with plastic wrap, and let marinate in the refrigerator for at least 2 hours or overnight, turning once or twice.

2 Turn the chicken pieces skin side up, sprinkle over the remaining whole garlic cloves, and place the lemon skins, cut side down, on top. Cook the chicken in a preheated oven, 400°F, for 45 minutes, or until golden brown, cooked through, and tender. Stir in the parsley, season to taste with salt and pepper, and serve garnished with sprigs of parsley.

STUDENT TIP

It's cheaper to buy a whole chicken and cut it into portions. You could ask the butcher to do this for you or, if you have a good-quality sharp knife, you could do it yourself. It's simply a case of cutting the chicken in half, then separating the legs from the breast and cutting the legs from the thighs—this will give you six portions ready for the pot.

CHICKEN with *Spring Herbs*

1 cup mascarpone cheese
1 handful of chervil, finely chopped
½ bunch of parsley, finely chopped
2 tablespoons chopped mint
4 boneless, skin-on chicken breasts
2 tablespoons butter
scant 1 cup white wine
salt and pepper
garlic bread, to serve (optional)

Serves **4**
Prep time **15 minutes**
Cooking time **25 minutes**

1 Mix together the mascarpone and herbs in a bowl and season well with salt and pepper. Lift the skin away from each chicken breast and spread a quarter of the mascarpone mixture on each breast. Replace the skin and smooth carefully over the mascarpone mixture. Season with salt and pepper.

2 Place the chicken breasts in a baking dish, dot with the butter, and pour the wine around it. Roast the chicken in a preheated oven, 350°F, for 20–25 minutes until golden and crisp and cooked through. Serve with garlic bread, if desired.

AFFORDABILITY 3

CHICKEN, CHORIZO & BLACK BEAN STEW

scant 1½ cups dried black
  beans, soaked in a bowl of
  cold water overnight
8 bone-in, skinless chicken
  thighs
5 oz chorizo sausage, cut into
  small chunks
1 onion, sliced
1 fennel bulb, trimmed and
  chopped
2 green bell peppers, cored,
  seeded, and cut into chunks
1 teaspoon saffron threads
salt and pepper

Serves **4-5**
Prep time **15 minutes, plus**
  overnight soaking
Cooking time **2½ hours**

1 Drain the beans and transfer to a large ovenproof
casserole. Cover with plenty of fresh cold water. Bring
to a boil and boil for 10 minutes. Drain the beans and
return to the pan.

2 Add the chicken, chorizo, onion, fennel, and green bell
peppers and sprinkle in the saffron. Almost cover the
ingredients with cold water and bring to a simmer. Cover
and cook in a preheated oven, 325°F, for 2 hours, or until
the beans are very soft.

3 Using a slotted spoon, drain a couple of spoonfuls of the
beans and transfer them to a bowl. Mash the beans with
a fork and then return to the casserole, stirring gently
to thicken the juices. Season to taste with salt and
pepper and serve.

VARIATION
For chorizo with chickpeas, fry 5 oz diced chorizo sausage in
a large saucepan. Add 2 thinly sliced shallots, 2 x 13 oz cans
chopped tomatoes, 2 x 13 oz cans chickpeas, rinsed and
drained, ¼ cup raisins, 2 tablespoons sherry vinegar,
1 tablespoon honey, and 1 teaspoon paprika. Bring to a
simmer, then reduce the heat, cover, and cook gently
for 30 minutes. Season to taste with salt and pepper
and serve.

AFFORDABILITY 2

ROAST CHICKEN WITH
BUTTERNUT SQUASH

1 lb butternut squash, peeled, seeded, and cut into thin slices
1 red onion, sliced
4 bone-in, skin-on chicken breasts
2 tablespoons olive oil
1 tablespoon balsamic vinegar
¼ cup walnut halves
8 sage leaves
salt and pepper

To serve
crusty bread
green salad

Serves **4**
Prep time **10 minutes**
Cooking time **20-25 minutes**

1 Arrange the squash, onion, and chicken in a roasting pan. Drizzle over the oil, season to taste with salt and pepper, and toss to make sure everything is well coated in oil. Turn the chicken skin side up and roast in a preheated oven, 400°F, for 15 minutes.

2 Drizzle over the balsamic vinegar and sprinkle the walnuts and sage leaves around the chicken. Return to the oven for 5-10 minutes until the squash is tender and the chicken is cooked through. Serve with crusty bread and green salad.

VARIATION
For a chicken, butternut squash and goat cheese pasta, cook 2 cups peeled, seeded, and diced butternut squash in a large saucepan of lightly salted boiling water for 6 minutes. Add 1 lb fresh penne pasta and cook for another 3 minutes, or according to the package directions. Add 3 cups baby spinach leaves, then drain immediately and return the pasta and vegetables to the pan. Stir in ⅓ cup soft goat cheese and 1 ready-cooked chicken breast, torn into shreds, then season to taste with salt and pepper and serve topped with coarsely chopped walnuts.

AFFORDABILITY

Chicken RATATOUILLE

1 Cut a couple of slashes across each chicken thigh and season with salt and pepper. Heat the oil in a large, deep skillet, add the chicken, and cook over high heat for 5 minutes, turning occasionally.

2 Add the onion, eggplant, green and red bell peppers, zucchini, and garlic and cook for 10 minutes, or until softened, adding a little water if the mixture becomes too dry.

3 Pour in the tomatoes, add the sugar, and season to taste with salt and pepper. Bring to a boil, stirring, then reduce the heat, cover, and simmer for 15 minutes, stirring occasionally. Stir in the basil and serve.

8 small skinless chicken thighs
1 tablespoon olive oil
1 onion, chopped
1 eggplant, cut into bite-size chunks
1 green bell pepper, cored, seeded, and cut into bite-size chunks
1 red bell pepper, cored, seeded, and cut into bite-size chunks
2 zucchini, chopped
1 garlic clove, crushed
13 oz can chopped tomatoes
pinch of superfine sugar
handful of basil leaves, coarsely torn
salt and pepper

Serves **4**
Prep time **15 minutes**
Cooking time **30 minutes**

AFFORDABILITY
1

PAPRIKA CHICKEN & PEPPERS

1   Heat the oil in a large skillet, add the chicken, and stir-fry over high heat for 5 minutes. Add the garlic paste, paprika, mixed bell peppers, and tomato paste and cook, stirring, for 3 minutes.

2   Stir in the sour cream, season to taste with salt and pepper, and heat through. Serve with cooked tagliatelle.

1 tablespoon sunflower oil
13 oz chicken mini-fillets
1 teaspoon garlic paste
1 tablespoon paprika
6 oz frozen sliced mixed bell peppers
1 tablespoon tomato paste
$2/3$ cup sour cream
salt and pepper
cooked tagliatelle, to serve

Serves **4**
Prep time **5 minutes**
Cooking time **10 minutes**

STUDENT TIP

Always label your freezer food clearly ... unless you don't mind having a lucky dip dinner in a couple of weeks' time. Buy a batch of freezer bags, stickers, and a suitable marker pen and keep them somewhere handy so you can batch up leftovers quickly.

Tandoori CHICKEN & ONIONS

1 Line a baking sheet with foil and set a wire rack on top. Make 3 slashes across each chicken breast. Mix together the yogurt, garlic, ginger, and tandoori paste in a bowl and season well with salt and pepper. Add the chicken and rub the tandoori mixture all over the chicken. Let marinate for 5-10 minutes.

2 Toss the chicken with the onion and oil, then arrange on the rack. Bake in a preheated oven, 450°F, for 7 minutes.

3 Add the tomatoes, sprinkle over the butter, and return to the oven for another 5-10 minutes until the chicken is charred and cooked through. Serve with lime wedges, raita, and warm naan breads.

4 skinless chicken breast fillets
scant ½ cup plain yogurt
1 garlic clove, crushed
2 teaspoons finely grated fresh ginger root
2 tablespoons tandoori curry paste
1 onion, cut into wedges
2 tablespoons vegetable oil
2 tomatoes, quartered
1 tablespoon butter, cut into small pieces
salt and pepper

To serve
lime wedges
ready-made raita
warm naan breads

Serves **4**
Prep time **10 minutes, plus marinating**
Cooking time **15-20 minutes**

Chicken & tomato
POLENTA PIE

2 tablespoons olive oil
10 oz skinless chicken breast
  fillets, diced
2 garlic cloves, finely chopped
13 oz can chopped tomatoes
1 teaspoon tomato paste
pinch of dried red pepper flakes
handful of chopped basil
1 zucchini, sliced
1 lb ready-cooked polenta, cut
  into ½ inch slices
⅓ cup Parmesan cheese, grated
salt and pepper

Serves **4**
Prep time **10 minutes**
Cooking time **30-35 minutes**

1 Heat the oil in a shallow ovenproof casserole. Add the chicken, season to taste with salt and pepper, and cook for 3-4 minutes until starting to turn golden. Lift out with a slotted spoon onto a plate.

2 Add the garlic to the casserole and cook for 1 minute, then pour in the tomatoes and stir in the tomato paste, red pepper flakes, and basil. Bring to a boil, then reduce the heat and simmer for 10 minutes.

3 Return the chicken to the casserole, add the zucchini, and cook for another 5-10 minutes until the chicken is cooked through.

4 Arrange the polenta slices on top of the chicken mixture, then sprinkle over the Parmesan. Cook under a preheated hot broiler for 5 minutes, or until golden and bubbling.

Herby roast TURKEY BREAST

handful of chopped rosemary
handful of chopped parsley
2 tablespoons butter, softened
1 lb 10 oz turkey breast joint
6 garlic cloves
scant ¼ cup dry white wine
scant ¼ cup hot chicken stock
   (see page 11 for homemade)
4 slices of pancetta
2 x 13 oz cans lima beans,
   rinsed and drained
handful of sunblush tomatoes,
   coarsely chopped
scant ¼ cup heavy cream
salt and pepper

Serves **4**
Prep time **10 minutes**
Cooking time **30 minutes**

1 Mix together the rosemary, three-quarters of the parsley, and the butter in a bowl. Smear the flavored butter over the turkey joint. Season to taste with salt and pepper.

2 Place the turkey in a roasting pan with the whole garlic cloves, pour the wine and stock into the pan, and arrange the pancetta on top of the turkey. Roast in a preheated oven, 425°F, for 25 minutes.

3 Add the beans, tomatoes, and cream to the roasting pan, topping off with a little water if necessary. Season to taste with salt and pepper, then return to the oven for another 3-5 minutes until the turkey is cooked through and the beans are warm.

4 Cut the turkey into slices and arrange on serving plates with the crispy pancetta and the beans, sprinkled with the remaining parsley.

VARIATION

For spaghetti with turkey, ham, and beans, cook 1 lb fresh spaghetti in a large saucepan of lightly salted boiling water according to the package directions. Add 1⅓ cups canned cannellini beans, rinsed and drained, for the last minute of the cooking time. Drain and then return the pasta and beans to the pan. Add 4 slices of ready-cooked turkey, cut into strips, 2 slices of ham, cut into strips, and a handful of chopped sunblush tomatoes. Stir in 4 tablespoons crème fraîche and 2 oz arugula. To serve, divide among serving plates and sprinkle over plenty of grated Parmesan cheese.

TURKEY, SWEET POTATO & COCONUT CURRY

1 Heat the oil in a large, shallow saucepan or skillet. Add the fennel and onion and fry gently, stirring frequently, for 5 minutes. Add the turkey and garlic and fry for another 5 minutes, or until the ingredients are beginning to lightly brown.

2 Stir in the stock, oregano or thyme, tomato paste, and sweet potatoes. Bring to a gentle simmer, cover, and cook for 15 minutes.

3 Add the creamed coconut and jalapeños to the pan. The coconut will melt into the juices. Cover and cook for another 25 minutes, stirring occasionally, until the potatoes are tender. Add a dash of water toward the end of the cooking time if the sauce starts to dry out.

4 Season to taste with salt, if necessary. Serve in bowls, sprinkled with chopped cilantro.

COOKING TIP
The fresh cilantro adds another burst of flavor to the curry. To save wasting the rest of the pack, coarsely chop the cilantro and freeze in a small plastic freezer bag for another time.

2 tablespoons vegetable oil
1 fennel bulb, chopped
1 red onion, chopped
11½ oz lean turkey breast, cut into small chunks
4 garlic cloves, finely chopped
2 cups chicken or vegetable stock (see pages 11 or 15 for homemade)
1 teaspoon dried oregano or thyme
2 tablespoons tomato paste
1½ lb sweet potatoes, scrubbed and cut into ¾ inch chunks
3½ oz creamed coconut, cut into a few pieces
1¼ oz jalapeños in brine, drained and chopped
salt
chopped cilantro, to garnish

Serves **4**
Prep time **20 minutes**
Cooking time **50 minutes**

AFFORDABILITY
2

PORK & LEEK *stew*

1 Season the pork with plenty of salt and pepper. Heat 1 tablespoon of the oil in a large ovenproof casserole and fry the pork in batches until browned on all sides, lifting out with a slotted spoon onto a plate.

2 Add the remaining oil to the casserole and gently fry the onion and leeks for 5 minutes. Return the pork to the pan, add the bay leaves and stock, and bring to a simmer. Stir in the pearl barley. Cover, reduce the heat to its lowest setting, and cook for about 1½ hours until the pork and barley are tender and the cooking juices have thickened.

3 Mix together the flour, suet, and a little salt and pepper in a bowl. Add the measured water and mix with a round-bladed knife to a soft dough, adding a dash more water if the mixture feels dry and crumbly, but don't make it too sticky.

4 Stir the prunes into the stew and season to taste with salt and pepper. Using a dessertspoon, place spoonfuls of the dumpling mixture on the surface of the stew, spacing them slightly apart. Cover again and cook gently for another 15-20 minutes until the dumplings have risen and have a fluffy texture. Serve in shallow bowls.

2 lb boneless lean pork, diced
2 tablespoons vegetable oil
1 large onion, chopped
1 lb leeks, trimmed, cleaned, and chopped
3 bay leaves
5 cups chicken or beef stock (see pages 11 or 98 for homemade)
scant ½ cup pearl barley
1 cup + 2 tablespoons self-rising flour
5 tablespoons beef or vegetable suet
about ½ cup cold water
1⅓ cups pitted prunes, halved
salt and pepper

Serves **4-5**
Prep time **25 minutes**
Cooking time **2 hours**

AFFORDABILITY

MEDITERRANEAN PORK STEW

AFFORDABILITY 2

1 Heat the oil in an ovenproof casserole and fry the pork for 4-5 minutes until browned on all sides. Lift out with a slotted spoon onto a plate.

2 Add the onion, garlic, and yellow bell pepper to the pan and fry for 2 minutes. Return the pork to the casserole together with all the remaining ingredients.

3 Bring to a boil, then reduce the heat, cover, and cook gently for 1 hour, or until the meat is tender. Garnish with sprigs of thyme and serve with garlic bread.

VARIATION
For a borlotti bean casserole, omit the pork and fry the onion, garlic, and yellow bell pepper in the oil as above, then stir in the artichoke hearts and tomatoes. Rinse and drain a 13 oz can borlotti beans and add to the casserole with the wine, olives, lemon zest, and herbs. Bring to a boil, then reduce the heat, cover, and cook gently for about 1 hour. Serve garnished with chopped parsley.

1 tablespoon olive oil
8 oz boneless lean pork, cut into chunks
1 red onion, cut into thin wedges
1 garlic clove, crushed
1 yellow bell pepper, cored, seeded, and chopped
8 artichoke hearts in oil, drained and quartered
7 oz can chopped tomatoes
scant ½ cup red wine
½ cup black olives, pitted
grated zest of 1 lemon
1 bay leaf
1 sprig of thyme, plus extra to garnish
garlic bread, to serve

Serves **2**
Prep time **10 minutes**
Cooking time **1 hour 10 minutes**

LOVELY LEFTOVERS

If the first thing that springs to mind when you think of leftovers is grabbing a slice of congealed pizza from the refrigerator the morning after a drinking session, think again. Leftover food offers another chance to enjoy a delicious meal; it will make your grocery budget stretch further and it's a great way to make the most of your freezer. If you are freezing your leftovers, make sure you have a stash of freezer bags, ties, and labels, or a collection of freezerproof containers ... and space in the freezer!

One-pot cooking is particularly suited to leftovers, as the food can be easily portioned into containers or freezer bags, labeled, and saved for another day. But, while it's quick and easy to simply reheat and serve a portion of a favorite meal, there are also lots of ways to transform your leftovers into a completely new dish. If you are planning to serve up a new incarnation of tonight's dinner, it's very important to cover and chill the leftover food in the refrigerator and to thoroughly reheat or cook it through before its next visit to the dinner table. Here are a few ideas to get you started.

CHILI CON CARNE

Chilling chili con carne overnight allows the flavors to really develop and some people would argue that it tastes better the next day. Reheat thoroughly and use as a filling for baked potatoes or roasted peppers. It also makes a great pizza topping.

RISOTTO

Crispy, melt-in-the-mouth risotto balls (or arancini to give them their correct Italian name) are the perfect way to use up any risotto that doesn't get devoured on its first outing. Take the leftover risotto from the refrigerator and stir in some chopped mozzarella, if you like. Dip the risotto balls in beaten egg and then roll them in bread crumbs. Heat vegetable oil in a large pan and cook the balls until they've turned an even golden brown.

CHICKEN

This is probably the most versatile one-pot leftover ingredient. Slice pot-roast chicken and use it as a filling for sandwiches and wraps; add it to pasta sauces or salads; make a chicken pie with ham and leeks or use chicken thighs for a curry or a risotto.

PORK CHOPS & POTATOES

2 tablespoons olive oil
4 large pork chops, about 8 oz each
4 oz smoked bacon in one piece, rind discarded, and diced
1 large onion, sliced
1½ lb potatoes, cut into 1 inch cubes
2 garlic cloves, chopped
2 teaspoons dried oregano
grated zest and juice of 1 lemon
1 cup chicken stock (see page 11 for homemade)
salt and pepper
thyme leaves, to garnish (optional)

Serves **4**
Prep time **10 minutes**
Cooking time **50 minutes**

1 Heat the oil in an ovenproof casserole and fry the pork chops until browned on both sides. Lift out with a slotted spoon onto a plate.

2 Add the bacon and onion to the pan and cook over medium heat, stirring, for 3-4 minutes until golden.

3 Stir the potatoes, garlic, oregano, and lemon zest into the pan. Pour over the stock and lemon juice and season lightly. Cook, uncovered, in a preheated oven, 350°F, for 20 minutes.

4 Arrange the chops on top of the potato mixture and return to the oven for another 20 minutes, or until the potatoes and pork chops are cooked through. Serve garnished with thyme leaves, if desired.

VARIATION

For pork chops with sweet potatoes and sage, cook the recipe above using 1½ lb sweet potatoes, peeled and cut into cubes, instead of the potatoes and 1 tablespoon chopped sage in place of the dried oregano.

HOISIN PORK *Stir-fry*

1 tablespoon hoisin sauce
1 tablespoon light soy sauce
1 tablespoon white wine
  vinegar
1 tablespoon vegetable oil
2 garlic cloves, sliced
1 teaspoon grated fresh
  ginger root
1 small red chile, seeded and
  sliced
8 oz pork tenderloin, thinly
  sliced
6 oz sugar snap peas
6 oz broccoli florets
2 tablespoons water
steamed rice, to serve

Serves **2**
Prep time **10 minutes**
Cooking time **10 minutes**

1 Combine the hoisin and soy sauces and vinegar in a mug and set aside.

2 Heat the oil in a wok until starting to smoke, add the garlic, ginger, and chile, and stir-fry over high heat for 10 seconds. Add the pork tenderloin and stir-fry for 2–3 minutes, or until golden. Lift out with a slotted spoon onto a plate.

3 Add the sugar snap peas and broccoli florets to the wok and stir-fry for 1 minute. Add the measured water and cook for another 1 minute.

4 Return the pork to the wok, add the hoisin mixture, and cook for 1 minute, or until the vegetables are cooked. Serve with steamed rice.

VARIATION
For roasted hoisin pork, make the hoisin mixture as above. Brush the sauce over 4 pieces of pork tenderloin, about 6 oz each, in a roasting pan and roast in a preheated oven, 400°F, for 15 minutes. Let rest for 5 minutes, then serve with steamed green vegetables and boiled rice.

AFFORDABILITY
2

SAUSAGE & ONION
TRAYBAKE

3 red onions, cut into wedges
3 red apples, cored and cut into
  6 wedges
7 oz baby carrots, scrubbed
3 potatoes, peeled and cut into
  small cubes
4 tablespoons olive oil
12 good-quality pork sausages
2 tablespoons chopped sage
1 tablespoon rosemary
3 tablespoons honey
salt and pepper

Serves **4**
Prep time **10 minutes**
Cooking time **20-25 minutes**

1 Sprinkle the onions, apples, carrots, and potatoes in a large roasting pan. Drizzle over the oil and toss well to lightly coat all the vegetables in the oil. Season generously with salt and pepper. Arrange the sausages in and around the vegetables, sprinkle over the herbs, and toss again.

2 Bake in a preheated oven, 400°F, for 20-22 minutes until golden and cooked through.

3 Remove from the oven and drizzle over the honey. Toss all the vegetables and sausages in the honey and serve.

VARIATION

For a quick pork, apple, and onion stir-fry, cut 8 oz pork tenderloin into very thin slices. Heat 2 tablespoons olive oil in a large wok or heavy skillet and stir-fry the pork over high heat for 2-3 minutes. Add 2 cored apples and 2 red onions, each cut into slim wedges, and stir-fry for 3-4 minutes until browned and softened. Add 1 tablespoon chopped sage leaves or rosemary and toss to mix. Serve with warm ciabatta and plenty of Dijon mustard.

CHORIZO & CAULIFLOWER CHEESE PIE

1 Layer up half the cauliflower, onion, chorizo, and parsnips in a pie dish or shallow ovenproof dish. Repeat with the remaining cauliflower, onion, chorizo, and parsnips and season with pepper—you probably won't need any salt. Spoon the cheese sauce on top.

2 Roll out the pastry until large enough to generously cover the top of the dish. (If the pastry sticks to the surface, dust with a sprinkling of flour). Brush the edges of the dish with water and position the pastry, pressing it firmly down on the rim of the dish. Trim off the excess, leaving a bit of an overhang as the pastry will shrink slightly as it cooks.

3 Make a hole in the center of the pie with the tip of a knife to let the steam escape. Decorate by pressing a fork all around the edges of the pie or by crimping the edges between your thumb and fingers.

4 Brush the top of the pie with beaten egg or milk to glaze (use your fingers or a piece of paper towel if you don't have a pastry brush). If desired, decorate the top of the pie with the pastry trimmings.

5 Bake in a preheated oven, 400°F, for about 1 hour or until the pastry is risen and golden and the vegetables feel tender when you press the tip of a knife down into the filling. Cover the pie with foil if it starts to overbrown before it's cooked through. Serve with seasonal green vegetables.

VARIATION
For a vegetarian version, omit the chorizo and sprinkle the vegetables with a finely chopped red chile before adding the cheese sauce. Alternatively, try a sprinkling of cumin seeds and a generous sprinkling of chopped cilantro.

1 cauliflower, cut into small pieces
1 large red onion, thinly sliced
4 oz chorizo sausage, cut into ½ inch dice
2 parsnips, thinly sliced
8 oz tub ready-made cheese sauce
1 lb puff pastry
pepper
beaten egg or milk, to glaze
seasonal green vegetables, to serve

Serves **4**
Prep time **20 minutes**
Cooking time **1 hour**

AFFORDABILITY 2

CHORIZO & CHICKPEA STEW

1 teaspoon olive oil
2 red onions, chopped
2 red bell peppers, cored, seeded, and chopped
3½ oz chorizo sausage, thinly sliced
1 lb cooked new potatoes, sliced
3 cups chopped plum tomatoes, or 13 oz can chopped tomatoes, drained
13 oz can chickpeas, rinsed and drained
2 tablespoons chopped parsley, to garnish
garlic bread, to serve

Serves **4**
Prep time **5 minutes**
Cooking time **20 minutes**

1 Heat the oil in a large skillet and fry the onions and red bell peppers over medium heat for 3–4 minutes. Add the chorizo and cook, turning frequently, for 2 minutes.

2 Stir the potatoes, tomatoes, and chickpeas into the pan and bring to a boil. Reduce the heat and cook gently for 10 minutes. Garnish with the chopped parsley and serve with garlic bread to mop up all the juices.

VARIATION

For a sausage and mixed bean stew, fry the onions and red bell peppers in the oil as above. Add 4 pork sausages instead of the chorizo to the pan and cook for 4–5 minutes until browned on all sides. Lift the sausages from the pan and cut each into 6 thick slices. Return to the pan and add the potato slices and tomatoes as above but replace the chickpeas with a 13 oz can mixed beans, rinsed and drained. Bring to a boil and cook as above. If you prefer a slightly hotter stew, add 1 seeded and chopped red chile when frying the onions and peppers.

AFFORDABILITY
1

PORK, APPLE & *Mustard*

2 tablespoons olive oil
2 tablespoons butter
1 large red onion, cut into slim
   wedges
2 red apples, cored and cut into
   slim wedges
1 lb 3 oz pork tenderloin, thinly
   sliced
1¼ cups hot chicken stock (see
   page 11 for homemade)
scant 1 cup crème fraîche
2 tablespoons Dijon mustard
2 tablespoons whole-grain
   mustard
6 tablespoons chopped parsley
mashed potatoes, to serve

Serves **4-6**
Prep time **10 minutes**
Cooking time **20 minutes**

1 Heat the oil and butter in a large skillet, add the onion
and apples, and cook over medium-high heat for
5 minutes, turning and stirring occasionally, until
golden and starting to soften. Lift out with a slotted
spoon onto a plate.

2 Add the pork to the pan and cook over high heat for
5 minutes, or until golden and cooked through. Return
the onion and apples to the pan with the stock and bring
to a boil. Reduce the heat and simmer for 3 minutes,
or until the stock has reduced by half, then add the crème
fraîche and mustards and heat through for 2 minutes.
Stir in the parsley, then serve hot with mashed potatoes.

SWEET & SOUR
PORK

1 tablespoon vegetable oil
½ pineapple, skinned, cored, and cut into bite-size chunks
1 onion, cut into chunks
1 orange bell pepper, cored, seeded, and cut into chunks
12 oz pork tenderloin, cut into strips
3½ oz snow peas, halved lengthwise
6 tablespoons tomato ketchup
2 tablespoons soft light brown sugar
2 tablespoons white wine or malt vinegar
cooked egg noodles, to serve (optional)

Serves **4**
Prep time **10 minutes**
Cooking time **20 minutes**

1 Heat the oil in a large wok and stir-fry the pineapple over very high heat for 3–4 minutes until browned in places. Lift out with a slotted spoon onto a plate.

2 Add the onion and orange bell pepper to the wok and cook over high heat, stirring frequently, for 5 minutes, or until softened. Add the pork and stir-fry for 5 minutes, or until browned and cooked through.

3 Return the pineapple to the wok together with the snow peas and cook, stirring occasionally, for 2 minutes.

4 Meanwhile, mix together the tomato ketchup, sugar, and vinegar in a mug. Pour over the pork mixture, toss, and cook for another 1 minute to heat the sauce through. Serve immediately, with cooked egg noodles, if desired.

Liver & ONIONS

3½ tablespoons butter
2 tablespoons olive oil
2 large onions, thinly sliced
1¼ lb calves' liver, thinly sliced
(ask your butcher to slice as
thinly as possible)
2 tablespoons finely chopped
parsley, to garnish
salt and pepper

Serves **4**
Prep time **10 minutes**
Cooking time **40-45 minutes**

1 Melt half the butter with the oil in a large heavy skillet with a tight-fitting lid. Add the onions and season with salt and pepper, then cover, reduce the heat to its lowest setting, and cook, stirring occasionally, for 35-40 minutes until very soft and golden. Lift out with a slotted spoon onto a plate.

2 Increase the heat to high and melt the remaining butter in the pan. Season the liver with salt and pepper. Once the butter starts foaming, add the liver and cook for 1-2 minutes until browned. Turn over the liver, return the onions to the pan, and cook for another 1 minute. Serve garnished with the chopped parsley.

AFFORDABILITY
1

CELERIAC & BACON BAKE

AFFORDABILITY
1

1 Cut away the skin from the celeriac until you have about 1 lb 3 oz of flesh. Cut the flesh into manageable pieces, about the size of the potatoes. Slice the celeriac and potatoes as thinly as possible.

2 Layer up half the celeriac and potatoes in a shallow ovenproof dish, seasoning lightly with pepper as you go. Arrange the bacon and onion on top. Sprinkle with half the cheddar then layer up the remaining celeriac and potatoes.

3 Pour over the stock, then the cream, and sprinkle with the remaining cheddar. Cover with foil and bake in a preheated oven, 350°F, for 30 minutes. Remove the foil and bake for another 45 minutes, or until the surface is bubbling and golden and the vegetables are tender. Serve with a mixed leaf salad.

1 small celeriac, about 1½ lb
10 oz baking potatoes
3½ oz smoked lean bacon, diced
1 large onion, chopped
2¾ cups grated cheddar cheese
⅔ cup chicken or vegetable stock (see pages 11 or 15 for homemade)
scant 1 cup heavy cream
pepper
mixed leaf salad, to serve

Serves **4**
Prep time **25 minutes**
Cooking time **1¼ hours**

BACON, PEA & ZUCCHINI *Risotto*

3½ tablespoons butter
generous ½ cup diced lean bacon
1½ cups risotto rice
scant ½ cup dry white wine (optional)
3½ cups hot chicken or vegetable stock (see pages 11 or 15 for homemade) (add an extra scant ½ cup if not using wine)
2 zucchini, about 11 oz in total, coarsely grated
1⅔ cups frozen peas, defrosted
1 small bunch of basil, shredded (optional)
salt and pepper
grated Parmesan cheese, to serve

Serves **4**
Prep time **5 minutes**
Cooking time **30 minutes**

1 Melt the butter in a large skillet or saucepan and cook the bacon over medium heat for 6-7 minutes until golden. Lift out half of the bacon with a slotted spoon onto a plate.

2 Add the rice to the pan and stir well. Pour in the wine, if using, and stock. Bring to a boil, then simmer gently for 15-18 minutes, stirring as often as possible, until the rice is tender and creamy. Stir in the zucchini and peas for the final 2-3 minutes of the cooking time.

3 Season with salt and pepper, then spoon the risotto into 4 serving bowls. Sprinkle over the reserved bacon and the basil, if using. Serve sprinkled with grated Parmesan.

Spicy SAUSAGE & TOMATO

AFFORDABILITY **1**

1 Heat the oil in a large skillet, add the sausages, and fry over high heat for 3-4 minutes until browned. Add the chile, garlic, onion, and red pepper flakes and fry for another 1-2 minutes.

2 Stir in the tomatoes, sugar, and rosemary and bring to a boil, then reduce the heat to medium and cook for 8-10 minutes. Season with salt and pepper. Garnish with the chopped parsley, then serve with cooked pasta and grated Parmesan to sprinkle over.

2 tablespoons olive oil
8 thick, spicy Italian sausages, cut into ¾ inch pieces
1 red chile, seeded and finely chopped
4 garlic cloves, finely chopped
1 onion, finely chopped
1 teaspoon dried red pepper flakes
13 oz can chopped tomatoes with herbs
1 teaspoon superfine sugar
2 teaspoons chopped rosemary
salt and pepper
4 tablespoons chopped parsley, to garnish

To serve
cooked pasta, such as penne
1½ cups Parmesan cheese, grated

Serves **4**
Prep time **10 minutes**
Cooking time **20 minutes**

SEARED PORK CHOPS
WITH CHILI CORN

1 Heat 1 tablespoon of the oil in a large skillet. Season the chops to taste with salt and pepper and cook in the pan for 5-7 minutes on each side until golden and cooked through. Remove from the pan and keep warm while you cook the chili corn.

2 Add the remaining oil to the pan, followed by the corn. Cook for 2 minutes, or until starting to brown, then stir in the scallions and chile and cook for another 1 minute. Stir in the crème fraîche and lime zest and season to taste with salt and pepper. Sprinkle over the chopped cilantro and serve with the pork chops.

VARIATION

For ham and corn melts, spread scant ½ cup cream cheese over 4 wheat tortillas. Tear up 4 slices of ham and sprinkle on top with ½ cup canned corn kernels and ¼ cup grated cheddar cheese. Place another tortilla on top of each, then cook under a preheated hot broiler for 3 minutes. Carefully turn over and cook for another 2-3 minutes until the cheese has melted inside.

2 tablespoons olive oil
4 pork chops
scant 1½ cups fresh or canned
   corn kernels
2 scallions, thinly sliced
1 red chile, chopped
5 tablespoons crème fraîche
finely grated zest of 1 lime
salt and pepper
handful of chopped cilantro, to
   garnish

Serves **4**
Prep time **5 minutes**
Cooking time **15-20 minutes**

BEEF &
PICKLED ONION
Stew

3 tablespoons all-purpose flour
2 lb chuck or braising steak, cut into large chunks
2 tablespoons olive oil
1 lb jar pickled onions, drained
2 carrots, thickly sliced
1¼ cups beer
2½ cups beef stock (see page 98 for homemade)
4 tablespoons tomato paste
1 tablespoon Worcestershire sauce
2 bay leaves
salt and pepper
chopped parsley, to garnish

Serves **4**
Prep time **10 minutes**
Cooking time **2¼ hours**

1   Season the flour with salt and pepper on a plate. Coat the beef with the flour.

2   Heat the oil in a large ovenproof casserole and fry the beef in batches until browned on all sides, lifting out with a slotted spoon onto a plate.

3   Return all the beef to the pan. Stir in the pickled onions and carrots, then gradually blend in the beer and stock. Bring to a boil, stirring, then add the tomato paste, Worcestershire sauce, and bay leaves, and season with salt and pepper to taste.

4   Cover and cook in a preheated oven, 325°F, for 2 hours, stirring halfway through, until the beef and vegetables are tender. Garnish with the chopped parsley and serve immediately.

COOKING TIP
If you don't have an ovenproof casserole use a saucepan for frying off, then transfer to a casserole or any shallow ovenproof dish.

AFFORDABILITY
2

Beef GOULASH

4 tablespoons olive oil
3 lb chuck or braising steak, cut into large chunks
2 onions, sliced
2 red bell peppers, cored, seeded, and diced
1 tablespoon smoked paprika
2 tablespoons chopped marjoram
1 teaspoon caraway seeds
4 cups beef stock (see tip for homemade)
5 tablespoons tomato paste
salt and pepper
French bread, to serve

....

Serves **8**
Prep time **10 minutes**
Cooking time **2-2½ hours**

....

1 Heat the oil in an ovenproof casserole and fry the beef in batches until browned on all sides, lifting out with a slotted spoon onto a plate.

2 Add the onions and red bell peppers to the pan and cook gently for 10 minutes, or until softened. Stir in the paprika, marjoram, and caraway seeds and cook, stirring, for 1 minute.

3 Return the beef to the pan. Add the stock and tomato paste, season to taste with salt and pepper, and bring to a boil, stirring. Reduce the heat, cover, and cook gently for 1½-2 hours. If the sauce needs thickening, uncover for the final 30 minutes of the cooking time. Serve with French bread.

COOKING TIP

For a homemade beef stock, place 1½ lb shin of beef, cut into chunks, in a large saucepan and add 2 chopped onions, 2-3 chopped carrots, 2 coarsely chopped celery stalks, 1 bay leaf, 1 bouquet garni, 4-6 black peppercorns, and 7⅔ cups cold water. Slowly bring to a boil, then reduce the heat, cover with a well-fitting lid, and simmer gently for 2 hours, skimming off any scum that rises to the surface. Strain through a fine strainer, discarding the solids, and let cool. Cover and store in the refrigerator for up to several days or freeze for up to 6 months. This makes about 5 cups.

AFFORDABILITY 2

BEEF & POTATO *hash*

1 Heat 1 tablespoon of the oil in a large heavy skillet with a lid and fry the beef for 10 minutes, breaking up the meat with a wooden spoon and stirring until browned and all the moisture has evaporated. Push the meat to one side of the pan, add the remaining oil, fennel, and celery and fry for 5 minutes, or until softened.

2 Blend the cornstarch with a little of the stock in a mug, pour into the pan, and stir to thicken. Add the remaining stock, tomato paste, potatoes, and star anise and bring to a simmer, stirring. Reduce the heat, cover, and cook gently for about 30 minutes until the potatoes are tender, stirring occasionally and adding a dash more water if the pan becomes dry.

3 Stir in the soy sauce and sugar and cook for another 5 minutes, uncovered if necessary to thicken the juices. Season to taste with salt and pepper and stir in the cilantro just before serving.

ACCOMPANIMENT TIP
For a watercress salad, to serve as an accompaniment, remove any tough stalks from 3½ oz watercress. Peel ½ cucumber, cut in half lengthwise, scoop out the seeds, and thinly slice the flesh. Put the watercress and cucumber in a large bowl and sprinkle with ½ bunch of scallions, finely chopped. Whisk 3 tablespoons peanut or vegetable oil with 2 teaspoons rice vinegar, ½ teaspoon superfine sugar, and a little salt and pepper in a mug. Drizzle the dressing over the salad.

2 tablespoons vegetable oil
3⅓ cups ground beef
1 fennel bulb, trimmed and chopped
2 celery stalks, chopped
2 teaspoons cornstarch
generous 1¾ cups beef stock (see page 98 for homemade)
3 tablespoons tomato paste
1 lb 7 oz waxy potatoes, cut into ¾ inch chunks
4 star anise, broken into pieces and crushed using a mortar and pestle (or a rolling pin or empty wine bottle)
3 tablespoons soy sauce
1 tablespoon light brown sugar
½ cup coarsely chopped cilantro
salt and pepper

Serves **4**
Prep time **15 minutes**
Cooking time **50 minutes**

AFFORDABILITY

1

West Indian
BEEF & BEAN STEW

3 tablespoons sunflower oil
3½ cups ground beef
6 cloves
1 onion, finely chopped
2 tablespoons medium curry
  powder
2 carrots, peeled and cut into
  ½ inch cubes
2 celery stalks, diced
1 tablespoon thyme
2 garlic cloves, crushed
4 tablespoons tomato paste
2½ cups hot beef stock (see
  page 98 for homemade)
1 large potato, peeled and cut
  into ½ inch cubes
scant 1½ cups canned black
  beans, rinsed and drained
scant 1½ cups canned black-eye
  peas, rinsed and drained
salt and pepper
lemon wedges, to serve

Serves **4**
Prep time **15 minutes**
Cooking time **30 minutes**

AFFORDABILITY
1

1 Heat the oil in a large heavy saucepan, add the beef, and fry, stirring, over medium-high heat for 5–6 minutes until browned.

2 Add the cloves, onion, and curry powder and cook for 2–3 minutes until the onions are beginning to soften, then stir in the carrots, celery, thyme, garlic, and tomato paste.

3 Pour in the beef stock to just cover the meat and stir well, then add the potato and beans and bring to a boil. Reduce the heat slightly and simmer for 20 minutes, uncovered, or until the potatoes and beef are tender, then season to taste with salt and pepper. Ladle the stew into serving bowls and serve with lemon wedges.

STUDENT TIP

Student kitchens are a favorite hangout for germs, and dirty cloths are germ magnets. If you're unsure of when the dishcloths last had a wash, rinse and squeeze them, then lay out flat in the microwave and zap them for 2–3 minutes.

Rustic Lamb & POTATO CURRY

1. Heat the oil in a large heavy skillet with a lid and cook the onion and lamb over high heat, stirring frequently, for 5 minutes, or until the lamb is browned all over and the onion softened.

2. Add the chile, if using, and cook, stirring, for 1 minute. Stir in the curry paste and cook, stirring, for another 2 minutes. Add the tomatoes, stock, and potatoes and bring to a boil. Reduce the heat, cover, and simmer for 10 minutes, then remove the lid and cook for another 10 minutes, or until the lamb is cooked through and the potatoes are tender.

3. Remove from the heat, then sprinkle over the cilantro and spoon in the yogurt, ready to stir in and serve.

VARIATION

For a simple chicken curry, heat 1 tablespoon vegetable oil in a large heavy saucepan and cook 3 thinly sliced boneless, skinless chicken breasts, about 6 oz each, over high heat, stirring, for 3 minutes. Stir in a 13 oz jar korma curry sauce and 1 chopped tomato and bring to a boil. Add 4 cups baby spinach leaves, then reduce the heat, cover, and simmer for 5 minutes, or until the chicken is cooked through. Serve with lightly toasted naan breads.

2 tablespoons vegetable oil
1 large onion, coarsely chopped
1¼ lb lean lamb, cut into cubes
1 small green chile, coarsely chopped (optional)
4 tablespoons korma curry paste
2 x 13 oz cans chopped tomatoes
1¼ cups chicken stock (see page 11 for homemade)
2 unpeeled potatoes, coarsely cut into cubes
¼ cup coarsely chopped cilantro
⅔ cup plain yogurt

Serves **4**
Prep time **15 minutes**
Cooking time **30 minutes**

POLLOCK
& Lentils

1. Heat 2 tablespoons of the oil in an ovenproof casserole and gently fry the onion for 6-8 minutes until lightly browned. Add the garlic and rosemary, savory, or thyme and cook for about 2 minutes.

2. Stir the lentils into the pan with the tomatoes, sugar, and stock. Bring to a simmer, then cover and cook in a preheated oven, 350°F, for 10 minutes. Check over the fish for any stray bones and cut into 8 pieces. Season with salt and pepper.

3. Stir the parsley and anchovies into the pan. Nestle the fish down into the lentils and drizzle the fish with the remaining oil. Cover again and return to the oven for another 25 minutes, or until the fish is cooked through. Serve with spoonfuls of garlic mayonnaise.

VARIATION

For a salsa verde sauce, to serve as an alternative accompaniment to the garlic mayonnaise, coarsely chop 1 cup parsley and ½ cup basil and place in a food processor with 1 coarsely chopped garlic clove, scant ¼ cup pitted green olives, 1 tablespoon rinsed and drained capers in brine, and ½ teaspoon Dijon mustard. Process until finely chopped. Add 1 tablespoon lemon juice and ½ cup olive oil and process to make a thick sauce. Season to taste with salt and pepper, adding a dash more lemon juice, if desired, for extra tang.

4 tablespoons olive oil
1 onion, finely chopped
4 garlic cloves, crushed
2 teaspoons finely chopped
  rosemary, savory, or thyme
13 oz can green lentils, rinsed
  and drained
13 oz can chopped tomatoes
2 teaspoons superfine sugar
⅔ cup fish stock (see page 104
  for homemade)
1¼ lb skinless pollock fillets
4 tablespoons chopped parsley
2 oz can anchovy fillets,
  drained and chopped
salt and pepper
garlic mayonnaise, to serve

Serves **4**
Prep time **15 minutes**
Cooking time **50 minutes**

Mackerel & Sesame
NOODLES

1 Put the mackerel in a bowl with the teriyaki sauce and toss to coat the fish with the sauce.

2 Warm the oil in a saucepan, then add the sesame seeds, scallions, garlic, and beans and heat through gently for 2 minutes.

3 Pour in the stock and bring to a gentle simmer. Cover and cook for 5 minutes.

4 Stir the mackerel, noodles, sugar, and lime juice into the pan and cook gently for 2 minutes, or until the mackerel is cooked and the broth is hot. Serve immediately.

COOKING TIP

For homemade fish stock, melt 1 tablespoon butter in a large saucepan and gently fry 2 lb white fish bones and trimmings until the trimmings have turned opaque. Add a quartered onion, 2 coarsely chopped celery stalks, a handful of parsley, several lemon slices, and 1 teaspoon peppercorns. Cover with cold water and bring to a gentle simmer. Cook very gently for 30–35 minutes. Strain through a strainer and let cool. Cover and chill for up to 2 days or freeze for up to 3 months.

2 large mackerel fillets, about 4 oz each, cut into pieces
2 tablespoons teriyaki sauce
2 teaspoons sesame oil
1 tablespoon sesame seeds
½ bunch of scallions, chopped
1 garlic clove, very thinly sliced
3½ oz green beans, trimmed and diagonally sliced
1¾ cups fish stock (see tip for homemade)
5 oz package medium straight-to-wok rice noodles
1 teaspoon superfine sugar
2 teaspoons lime juice

Serves **2**
Prep time **10 minutes**
Cooking time **12 minutes**

AFFORDABILITY 2

SMOKED HADDOCK
Cannelloni

1 Lightly grease an ovenproof dish with butter. Place the haddock in a bowl, pour over the measured water, and let stand for 3 minutes. Drain, reserving the water, and break up the fish.

2 Place the watercress in a strainer and pour over boiling water until it has wilted. Lay the watercress on a paper towel and squeeze to get rid of excess water. Coarsely chop the watercress, then mix it with the haddock and 2 tablespoons of the crème fraîche.

3 Divide the haddock mixture among the lasagna sheets, arranging it in a strip down the middle. Roll up the pasta and arrange snugly, seam side down, in the prepared ovenproof dish.

4 Mix together the remaining crème fraîche with the haddock soaking water in a mug, season with salt and pepper, and pour over the top of the pasta.

5 Sprinkle the bread crumbs over the pasta, cover the dish with foil, and bake in a preheated oven, 400°F, for 20 minutes. Remove the foil and cook under a preheated hot broiler until the bread crumbs are golden.

butter, for greasing
13 oz skinless smoked haddock
 fillet, cut into pieces
1¼ cups boiling water
10 oz watercress
scant 1 cup crème fraîche
8 fresh lasagna sheets
²/₃ cup dried bread crumbs
salt and pepper

Serves **4**
Prep time **15 minutes, plus
 standing**
Cooking time **20 minutes**

Spicy TUNA, TOMATO & OLIVE PASTA

AFFORDABILITY
1

11½ oz dried penne
2 x 13 oz cans tuna chunks in
   water, drained
2 red chiles, finely chopped
1 teaspoon dried red pepper
   flakes
2 cups pitted black olives
8 oz tub sunblush tomatoes in
   oil
salt and pepper
chopped parsley, to garnish

Serves **4**
Prep time **10 minutes**
Cooking time **10 minutes**

1 Cook the pasta in a large saucepan of lightly salted boiling water according to the package directions until al dente.

2 Meanwhile, put the tuna in a large bowl and coarsely flake with a fork, then add the chiles, red pepper flakes, olives, and tomatoes with their oil.

3 Drain the pasta, add it to the tuna mixture, and toss to mix well, then season with salt and pepper. Spoon into serving bowls, garnish with chopped parsley, and serve.

STUDENT TIP

If it has a very long or nonexistent use-by date then buy it in bulk. Look out for BOGOF (buy one, get one free) and half-price offers on things like toilet paper, pasta, and other dried and canned goods.

BAKED COD
WITH TOMATOES & OLIVES

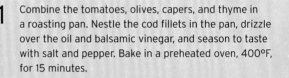

1½ cups cherry tomatoes, halved

1 cup pitted black olives

2 tablespoons capers in brine, drained

4 sprigs of thyme, plus extra to garnish

4 cod fillets, about 6 oz each

2 tablespoons extra virgin olive oil

2 tablespoons balsamic vinegar

salt and pepper

mixed leaf salad, to serve

Serves **4**
Prep time **5 minutes**
Cooking time **15 minutes**

1 Combine the tomatoes, olives, capers, and thyme in a roasting pan. Nestle the cod fillets in the pan, drizzle over the oil and balsamic vinegar, and season to taste with salt and pepper. Bake in a preheated oven, 400°F, for 15 minutes.

2 Transfer the fish, tomatoes, and olives to serving plates. Spoon the pan juices over the fish and serve immediately with a mixed leaf salad.

VARIATION
For steamed cod with lemon, arrange a cod fillet on each of 4 x 12 inch squares of foil. Top each with ½ teaspoon grated lemon zest, a squeeze of lemon juice, 1 tablespoon extra virgin olive oil, and salt and pepper to taste. Seal the edges of the foil together to form packages, transfer to a baking sheet, and cook in a preheated oven, 400°F, for 15 minutes. Remove from the oven and let rest for 5 minutes. Open the packages and serve sprinkled with chopped parsley.

AFFORDABILITY
3

PAELLA

2 lb live mussels
4 garlic cloves
1 small bunch of mixed herbs
$2/3$ cup dry white wine
8 cups hot chicken stock (see
   page 11 for homemade) or
   water
4 tablespoons olive oil
4 small cleaned squid, cut
   into rings
1 large onion, finely chopped
1 red bell pepper, cored, seeded,
   and chopped
4 large ripe tomatoes, skinned
   (see page 16), seeded, and
   chopped
12 skinless, boneless chicken
   thighs, cut into bite-size
   pieces
$2 2/3$ cups paella rice
large pinch of saffron threads,
   crumbled
1 cup fresh or frozen peas
12 large raw peeled shrimp
salt and pepper

Serves **6**
Prep time **40 minutes**
Cooking time **about 1½ hours**

1 Scrub the mussels in cold water. Scrape off any barnacles and pull away the dark hairy beards. Discard any with damaged shells or open ones that do not close when tapped firmly with a knife. Set aside.

2 Slice 2 of the garlic cloves and crush the remainder. Place the sliced garlic in a large heavy saucepan with the herbs, wine, and $2/3$ cup of the stock or water, and season well with salt and pepper. Tip in the mussels, cover, and cook, shaking the pan frequently, for 4–5 minutes until all the shells have opened. Lift out the mussels with a slotted spoon into a bowl, discarding any that remain closed. Strain the cooking liquid into a bowl and set aside.

3 Heat 2 tablespoons of the oil in the pan and fry the squid, stirring frequently, for 5 minutes. Add the onion, red bell pepper, and crushed garlic and cook gently for 5 minutes, or until softened. Add the mussel cooking liquid and tomatoes and season to taste. Bring to a boil, then reduce the heat and cook gently, stirring, for 15–20 minutes until thickened. Transfer to a bowl.

4 Heat the remaining oil in the pan, add the chicken, and fry for 5 minutes. Add the rice and cook, stirring, for 3 minutes.

5 Return the squid mixture to the pan, add one-third of the remaining stock and the saffron, and bring to a boil, stirring. Cover and simmer, adding stock a little at a time, for 30 minutes, or until the chicken is cooked, the rice is tender, and the liquid has been absorbed.

6 Taste and adjust the seasoning if needed. Add the peas and shrimp and simmer, for 5 minutes, adding a little more stock if required. Return the mussels to the pan, cover, and heat through for 5 minutes. Serve immediately.

ROAST SEA BASS
WITH POTATOES
& MUSHROOMS

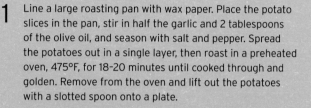

875 g (1¾ lb) potatoes, peeled
    and cut into 1 cm (½ inch)
    slices
2 garlic cloves, thinly sliced
3 tablespoons olive oil
250 g (8 oz) mixed wild
    mushrooms, sliced if large
4 sea bass fillets, about 175 g
    (6 oz) each
½ tablespoon chopped parsley
salt and pepper
extra virgin olive oil, for
    drizzling

Serves **4**
Prep time **10 minutes**
Cooking time **40-45 minutes**

1 Line a large roasting pan with wax paper. Place the potato slices in the pan, stir in half the garlic and 2 tablespoons of the olive oil, and season with salt and pepper. Spread the potatoes out in a single layer, then roast in a preheated oven, 475°F, for 18-20 minutes until cooked through and golden. Remove from the oven and lift out the potatoes with a slotted spoon onto a plate.

2 Place the pan on the stove, add the remaining oil, the mushrooms, and the remaining garlic, and cook over high heat, stirring frequently, until the mushrooms are tender. Season with salt and pepper and remove from the heat.

3 Return the roasted potatoes to the pan and stir well. Season the sea bass fillets with salt and pepper, then sit them, skin side up, on top of the potatoes. Sprinkle with the parsley and drizzle the fish with the remaining olive oil. Return to the oven and roast for 10-12 minutes until the fish is cooked through. Serve immediately with a drizzle of extra virgin olive oil.

AFFORDABILITY
3

Spicy SHRIMP & PEA PILAU

1. Heat the oil and butter in a heavy saucepan, add the onion, and cook over medium heat for 2-3 minutes until softened. Stir in the garlic and curry paste and cook for another 1-2 minutes until fragrant, then add the rice and stir to coat well.

2. Stir in the stock, peas, and lime zest, then season well with salt and pepper, and bring to a boil. Cover tightly, then reduce the heat to low and cook for 12-15 minutes until the liquid is absorbed and the rice is tender.

3. Remove from the heat, then stir in the lime juice, cilantro, and shrimp. Cover and let stand for a few minutes to let the shrimp heat through before serving.

VARIATION

For spicy shrimp and pea stir-fried rice, heat 2 tablespoons sunflower oil in a large wok or frying pan until hot, add 1 tablespoon medium curry paste, 13 oz ready-cooked peeled shrimp, scant 1²/₃ cups frozen peas, and 3½ cups ready-cooked basmati rice and stir-fry over high heat for 4-5 minutes until piping hot. Remove from the heat, season with salt and pepper, and stir in 6 tablespoons chopped cilantro. Serve immediately.

1 tablespoon sunflower oil
1 tablespoon butter
1 large onion, finely chopped
2 garlic cloves, finely chopped
1 tablespoon medium or hot curry paste
1¹/₃ cups basmati rice
2½ cups hot fish or vegetable stock (see pages 104 or 15 for homemade)
scant 2½ cups frozen peas
finely grated zest and juice of 1 large lime
²/₃ cup finely chopped cilantro
13 oz ready-cooked peeled shrimp
salt and pepper

Serves **4**
Prep time **10 minutes, plus standing**
Cooking time **20-25 minutes**

AFFORDABILITY 2

GOAT CHEESE & PEPPER *Lasagna*

11 oz can or jar pimientos,
   drained and coarsely chopped
6 tomatoes, skinned (see page
   16) and coarsely chopped
1 yellow bell pepper, cored,
   seeded, and finely chopped
2 zucchini, thinly sliced
⅔ cup sundried tomatoes,
   thinly sliced
½ cup sundried tomato pesto
1 cup basil
4 tablespoons olive oil
⅔ cup crumbled soft goat
   cheese
2½ cups ready-made cheese
   sauce (see tip for homemade)
5 oz dried egg lasagna
6 tablespoons grated Parmesan
   cheese
salt and pepper
mixed leaf salad, to serve

Serves **4**
Prep time **20 minutes, plus
   standing**
Cooking time **50 minutes–1 hour**

1 Place the pimientos in a bowl with the tomatoes, yellow pepper, zucchini, tomatoes, and pesto. Tear the basil leaves and add to the bowl with the oil and a little salt and pepper. Mix together thoroughly.

2 Spoon a quarter of the tomato mixture into a 1.5 quart shallow ovenproof dish and dot with a quarter of the goat cheese and 4 tablespoons of the cheese sauce. Cover with a third of the lasagna sheets in a layer, breaking them to fit where necessary. Repeat the layering, finishing with a layer of the tomato mixture and goat cheese.

3 Spoon over the remaining cheese sauce and sprinkle with the Parmesan. Bake in a preheated oven, 375°F, for 50 minutes–1 hour until deep golden. Let stand for 10 minutes before serving with a mixed leaf salad.

COOKING TIP
For a homemade cheese sauce, place 2 cups milk in a saucepan with 1 small onion and 1 bay leaf. Heat until just boiling, then remove from the heat and let infuse for 20 minutes. Strain the milk into a pitcher. Melt 3½ tablespoons butter in the cleaned saucepan, add 6 tablespoons all-purpose flour, and stir in quickly. Cook over medium heat, stirring, for 1–2 minutes, then remove from the heat and gradually whisk in the infused milk until blended. Return to the heat, bring gently to a boil, stirring, and cook for 2 minutes until the sauce has thickened. Remove from the heat and stir in 1⅓ cups grated cheddar or Gruyère cheese until melted.

Veggie
BEAN CHILI

(V)

1 Heat the oil in a large ovenproof casserole. Add the onion and cook for 5 minutes until softened, then add the red pepper, garlic, spices, and herbs and cook for 30 seconds. Pour in the tomatoes and season to taste with salt and pepper. Bring to a boil, then reduce the heat and simmer for 10 minutes.

2 Add the beans and corn to the pan and cook for another 3–4 minutes until heated through. Divide among serving bowls and top each portion with a spoonful of sour cream. Sprinkle with the chopped cilantro and grated cheese and serve with tortilla chips.

2 tablespoons vegetable oil
1 onion, finely chopped
1 red bell pepper, cored, seeded, and sliced
1 garlic clove, crushed
1 teaspoon ground cumin
1 teaspoon chipotle paste or a pinch of chili powder
1 teaspoon dried oregano
½ teaspoon ground coriander
13 oz can chopped tomatoes
13 oz can black beans, rinsed and drained
1 cup canned corn, drained

To serve
sour cream
handful of chopped cilantro
grated cheddar cheese
salt and pepper
tortilla chips

Serves **4**
Prep time **10 minutes**
Cooking time **20 minutes**

Middle Eastern
ZUCCHINI, TOMATO
& MINT CURRY

Vegan

2 tablespoons olive oil
2 onions, finely sliced
4 zucchini, cut into ½ inch
    cubes
2 x 13 oz cans peeled plum
    tomatoes
2 garlic cloves, crushed
1 teaspoon mild chili powder
¼ teaspoon ground turmeric
2 teaspoons dried mint
salt and pepper
small handful of finely chopped
    mint, to garnish

Serves **4**
Prep time **10 minutes**
Cooking time **25-30 minutes**

1 Heat the oil in a large heavy saucepan, add the onions, and cook over medium-low heat, stirring occasionally, for 6-8 minutes until softened. Add the zucchini and cook, stirring occasionally, for another 5-6 minutes until tender.

2 Increase the heat to medium, add the tomatoes and garlic, and cook for 10-12 minutes until the sauce is thickened. Stir in the chili powder, turmeric, and dried mint and cook for another 2-3 minutes. Season well with salt and pepper. Ladle the curry into serving bowls and garnish with the chopped mint.

AFFORDABILITY
1

SPICY GREEN BEAN,
POTATO & PESTO
LINGUINI

1 Cook the potatoes in a large saucepan of lightly salted
boiling water for 10-12 minutes until just tender, adding
the beans and linguine 4 minutes before the end of the
cooking time. Drain well, then return to the pan.

2 Mix together the chiles and pesto in a mug, then
season well with salt and pepper. Spoon into the pasta
mixture and toss to mix well. Divide among serving
bowls and serve with grated pecorino cheese to
sprinkle over.

7 oz potatoes, peeled and cut
    into small cubes
7 oz green beans, trimmed and
    halved
11½ oz fresh linguine
2 red chiles, finely chopped
1¼ cups store-bought fresh
    green pesto
salt and pepper
grated pecorino cheese,
    to serve

Serves **4**
Prep time **10 minutes**
Cooking time **15 minutes**

AFFORDABILITY
2

Creamy Chili & ZUCCHINI

1 Heat the oil and butter in a large skillet. Add the chiles, garlic, scallions, and zucchini and cook over medium-low heat for 10 minutes, or until softened.

2 Reduce the heat to low, add the lime zest, and gently cook for 3-4 minutes, then add the cream cheese and mix together until the cheese melts. Season to taste with salt and pepper, stir in the parsley, and serve with cooked pasta.

1 tablespoon olive oil
1 tablespoon butter
2 red chiles, finely chopped
2 garlic cloves, finely chopped
4 scallions, very finely chopped
3 zucchini, coarsely grated
finely grated zest of 1 lime
$2/3$ cup cream cheese
small handful of parsley, chopped
salt and pepper
cooked pasta, such as pennette or other short-shaped pasta, to serve

Serves **4**
Prep time **15 minutes**
Cooking time **15 minutes**

STUDENT TIP

Price comparison websites help you quickly locate the cheapest prices for your groceries. Forget about brand loyalty—follow the bargains to stretch your budget. Some grocery stores also now run a price-check on every shop and will apply the discount (if applicable) on your next visit.

Green veg CURRY

Vegan

AFFORDABILITY 1

1 tablespoon sunflower oil

3 tablespoons Thai green curry paste (see page 132 for homemade)

2 red chiles, seeded and finely sliced (optional)

14 oz can coconut milk

scant 1 cup vegetable stock (see page 15 for homemade)

6 kaffir lime leaves or 1 tablespoon finely grated lime zest

2 tablespoons soy sauce

1 tablespoon soft brown sugar

7 oz carrots, cut into thick sticks

8 oz butternut squash, peeled, seeded, and cut into ¾ inch cubes

3½ oz sugar snap peas

10 tablespoons finely chopped cilantro

juice of 1 lime

steamed jasmine rice, to serve

Serves **4**
Prep time **15 minutes**
Cooking time **15-20 minutes**

1 Heat the oil in a large nonstick saucepan. Add the curry paste and chiles, if using, and stir-fry for 2-3 minutes.

2 Stir in the coconut milk, stock, lime leaves or lime zest, soy sauce, sugar, carrots, and butternut squash. Simmer, uncovered for 6-8 minutes, stirring occasionally. Add the sugar snap peas and continue to simmer for 4-5 minutes.

3 Remove from the heat and stir in the cilantro and lime juice. Ladle the curry into serving bowls and serve with steamed jasmine rice.

PESTO PUFF TART

12 oz pack ready-rolled puff
  pastry
3 tablespoons store-bought
  fresh green pesto
1¾ cups yellow and red cherry
  tomatoes, halved
5 oz mixed antipasti
  (artichokes, roasted peppers,
  mushrooms, and eggplant),
  from a jar, drained
scant ½ cup crumbled goat
  cheese
basil leaves, to garnish

Serves **4**
Prep time **10 minutes**
Cooking time **15-20 minutes**

1   Lay the puff pastry on a baking sheet. Score a 1 inch margin
    around the edge and prick the base with a fork.

2   Top with the pesto, tomatoes, mixed antipasti, and goat cheese.
    Bake in a preheated oven, 400°F, for 15-20 minutes. Garnish
    with the basil leaves and serve.

AFFORDABILITY
2

Ranch-style EGGS Ⓥ

2 tablespoons olive oil
1 onion, finely sliced
1 red chile, seeded and finely
   chopped
1 garlic clove, crushed
1 teaspoon ground cumin
1 teaspoon dried oregano
13 oz canned cherry tomatoes
7 oz roasted red and yellow bell
   peppers in oil (from a jar),
   drained and coarsely chopped
4 eggs
salt and pepper
4 tablespoons finely chopped
   cilantro, to garnish

Serves **4**
Prep time **10 minutes**
Cooking time **15 minutes**

1 Heat the oil in a large skillet with a lid. Add the onion, chile, garlic, cumin, and oregano and fry gently for 5 minutes, or until softened.

2 Stir in the tomatoes and red and yellow bell peppers and cook for another 5 minutes, adding a splash of water if the sauce looks dry. Season well with salt and pepper.

3 Make 4 hollows in the sauce and break an egg into each hollow. Cover and cook for 5 minutes, or until the eggs are just set. Serve immediately, garnished with the chopped cilantro.

VARIATION

For a Mexican-style sauce, heat 2 tablespoons olive oil in a large skillet and add 1 finely chopped onion, 1 finely chopped red chile, 1 teaspoon each of ground cumin and dried oregano, 2 x 13 oz cans cherry tomatoes, and 7 oz chopped roasted red peppers in oil (from a jar, drained). Season with salt and pepper, bring to a boil, and cook over medium heat for 12-15 minutes. Stir in a small handful of chopped cilantro and serve over cooked pasta or rice.

AFFORDABILITY 1

OH SO QUICK & EASY

BALSAMIC
ROAST TOMATOES

CHICKEN BREASTS WITH
MASCARPONE & TOMATOES

THAI GREEN PORK CURRY

BOSTON BAKED BEANS

Sticky
LEMON CHICKEN

NOODLES

2 tablespoons vegetable oil
10 oz chicken fillets,
  cut into thin strips
7 oz Tenderstem broccoli
2 garlic cloves, crushed
2 teaspoons finely grated fresh
  ginger root
1 red chile, finely chopped
finely grated zest and juice
  of 1 lemon
1 tablespoon honey
2 teaspoons light soy sauce
10 oz ready-cooked egg noodles
handful of roasted cashew nuts,
  to garnish

Serves **4**
Prep time **10 minutes**
Cooking time **10 minutes**

1 Heat a large wok until smoking hot. Add the oil and swirl around the pan, then add the chicken and cook for 1 minute. Add the broccoli and cook for another 5 minutes, or until the chicken is nearly cooked through. Add the garlic, ginger, and chile to the wok and cook for 1 minute more. Then add the lemon zest and juice, honey, and soy sauce and toss around the pan.

2 Add the noodles and a splash of water and cook until heated through. Divide among serving bowls, garnish with the cashews, and serve.

CHICKEN BREASTS
WITH MASCARPONE & TOMATOES

4 tablespoons mascarpone
  cheese
4 teaspoons store-bought fresh
  green pesto
4 skinless chicken breast fillets
1¼ cups dried bread crumbs
3 tablespoons olive oil, plus
  extra for greasing
scant 1 cup cherry tomatoes
scant ¼ cup toasted pine nuts
salt and pepper
crusty bread, to serve (optional)

Serves **4**
Prep time **10 minutes**
Cooking time **15 minutes**

1 Mix together the mascarpone and pesto in a bowl. Cut a horizontal slit in the side of each chicken breast to form a pocket. Fill the pockets with the mascarpone mixture.

2 Spread out the bread crumbs on a plate. Season the chicken breasts with salt and pepper, rub them with 1 tablespoon of the oil, and then roll them in the bread crumbs until well coated.

3 Place the chicken breasts in a roasting pan, drizzle over another tablespoon of the oil, and bake in a preheated oven, 400°F, for 10 minutes.

4 Add the tomatoes to the pan, season with salt and pepper, and drizzle with the remaining oil. Return to the oven for another 5 minutes, or until the chicken is cooked through. Sprinkle over the pine nuts and serve with crusty bread, if desired.

AFFORDABILITY
3

Chicken drumstick
JAMBALAYA

1. Heat the oil in a large saucepan. Cut a few slashes across the thickest part of the drumsticks, add them to the pan, and fry over high heat for 5 minutes, turning occasionally. Add the onion, garlic, celery, chile, and green bell pepper and cook for another 2–3 minutes until softened.

2. Add the chorizo, fry briefly, then add the rice, stirring to coat the grains in the pan juices. Pour in the stock, add the bay leaf, and bring to a boil. Cover, reduce the heat, and simmer for 20 minutes, stirring occasionally, until the stock has been absorbed and the rice is tender.

3. Stir in the tomatoes and Tabasco sauce and season to taste with salt and pepper. Heat through for 3 minutes before serving.

1 tablespoon sunflower oil
8 skinless chicken drumsticks
1 onion, chopped
2 garlic cloves, crushed
2 celery stalks, sliced
1 red chile, seeded and chopped
1 green bell pepper, cored, seeded, and chopped
3 oz chorizo sausage, sliced
1⅓ cups long-grain rice
2 cups chicken stock (see page 11 for homemade)
1 bay leaf
3 tomatoes, cut into wedges
dash of Tabasco sauce
salt and pepper

Serves **4**
Prep time **15 minutes**
Cooking time **30 minutes**

AFFORDABILITY
2

French-style
CHICKEN STEW

1 Place the leek, chicken, potatoes, and carrot in a large saucepan. Pour in the stock and wine and season to taste with salt and pepper. Bring to a boil, then reduce the heat and simmer for 15 minutes, or until the chicken and vegetables are just cooked through.

2 Stir in the peas and crème fraîche and heat through. Sprinkle over the chopped tarragon and serve immediately.

1 leek, trimmed, cleaned, and sliced
4 boneless, skinless chicken thighs, cut into chunks
13 oz small new potatoes, halved
1 carrot, sliced
1¾ cups hot chicken stock (see page 11 for homemade)
scant ¼ cup dry white wine
scant 1 cup frozen peas, defrosted
2 tablespoons crème fraîche
salt and pepper
handful of chopped tarragon, to garnish

Serves **4**
Prep time **10 minutes**
Cooking time **20 minutes**

AFFORDABILITY
2

AFFORDABILITY
2

CHICKEN & SPINACH
Stew

1¼ lb skinless, boneless chicken thighs, thinly sliced
2 teaspoons ground cumin
1 teaspoon ground ginger
2 tablespoons olive oil
1 tablespoon tomato paste
2 x 13 oz cans cherry tomatoes
scant ⅓ cup raisins
1⅔ cups ready-cooked Puy lentils
1 teaspoon grated lemon zest
3 cups baby spinach leaves
salt and pepper
handful of chopped parsley, to garnish
steamed couscous or rice, to serve

Serves **4**
Prep time **10 minutes**
Cooking time **20 minutes**

1 Mix the chicken with the cumin and ginger in a bowl until well coated. Heat the oil in a large saucepan, then add the chicken and cook for 2–3 minutes until lightly browned.

2 Stir in the tomato paste, tomatoes, raisins, lentils, and lemon zest, season with salt and pepper, and simmer gently for about 12 minutes until thickened slightly and the chicken is cooked.

3 Add the spinach and stir until wilted. Ladle the stew into bowls, then garnish with the chopped parsley and serve with steamed couscous or rice.

Chicken & BEANS

1 tablespoon olive oil
2 boneless, skinless chicken
   breasts, each about 5 oz,
   thinly sliced
1 onion, thinly sliced
1 tablespoon molasses
1 tablespoon whole-grain
   mustard
1 tablespoon soft dark brown
   sugar
13 oz can chopped tomatoes
13 oz can baked beans
3 tablespoons chopped parsley
pepper
4 thick slices of whole-wheat
   toast, to serve

Serves **4**
Prep time **5 minutes**
Cooking time **10 minutes**

1 Heat the oil in a heavy saucepan and cook the chicken and onion over medium heat for 3-4 minutes.

2 Add the molasses, mustard, sugar, and tomatoes, bring to a boil, and simmer for 2 minutes. Stir in the beans and parsley and cook for another 1 minute, or until heated through.

3 Spoon the mixture onto the slices of whole-wheat toast, season with pepper, and serve immediately.

PORK & TOMATO RICE POT

1. Heat 1 tablespoon of the oil in a large, deep skillet with a lid. Add the pork tenderloin and cook over high heat for 3 minutes, or until golden and nearly cooked through. Lift out with a slotted spoon onto a plate.

2. Reduce the heat, add the remaining oil and the onion to the pan, and cook for 3 minutes, or until softened. Stir in the garlic and cook for 30 seconds, then stir in the rice and cook for 1 minute. Add the paprika and tomatoes, bring to a boil, and simmer for 2–3 minutes.

3. Pour in the stock, season to taste with salt and pepper, and cook for 12–15 minutes until there is just a little liquid left around the edges of the pan.

4. Lightly fork the spinach through the rice, arrange the pork on top, then cover and cook for another 3–4 minutes until the pork is cooked through. Serve with lemon wedges.

3 tablespoons olive oil
10 oz pork tenderloin, sliced
1 onion, finely chopped
3 garlic cloves, finely chopped
1⅓ cups paella rice
2 teaspoons smoked paprika
7 oz can chopped tomatoes
2¾ cups hot chicken stock (see page 11 for homemade)
2½ cups baby spinach leaves
salt and pepper
lemon wedges, to serve

Serves **4**
Prep time **10 minutes**
Cooking time **25–30 minutes**

AFFORDABILITY
2

THAI GREEN
PORK CURRY

2 tablespoons olive oil
4 boneless pork steaks, cut into
   bite-size pieces
2 tablespoons Thai green curry
   paste (see tip for homemade)
14 oz can coconut milk
3½ oz green beans
7 oz can water chestnuts,
   drained, rinsed, and cut
   in half
juice of 1 lime, or to taste
1 handful of cilantro leaves
boiled rice, to serve

Serves **4**
Prep time **10 minutes**
Cooking time **20 minutes**

1 Heat the oil in a large saucepan, add the pork, and cook, stirring, for 3-4 minutes until browned all over. Add the curry paste and cook, stirring, for 1 minute until fragrant.

2 Pour in the coconut milk, stir, and reduce the heat to a gentle simmer. Cook for 10 minutes, then add the beans and water chestnuts and cook for another 3 minutes.

3 Remove from the heat, add lime juice to taste, and stir through the cilantro. Serve immediately with boiled rice.

COOKING TIP
For homemade Thai green curry paste, put 15 small green chiles, 4 halved garlic cloves, 2 finely chopped lemon grass stalks, 2 torn lime leaves, 2 chopped shallots, 1¼ cups cilantro leaves, stalks, and roots, 1 inch piece of fresh ginger root, peeled and finely chopped, 2 teaspoons black peppercorns, 1 teaspoon pared lime zest, ½ teaspoon salt, and 1 tablespoon peanut oil into a food processor or blender and process to a thick paste. Alternatively, use a mortar and pestle to crush the ingredients, working in the oil at the end. Transfer the paste to an airtight container; it can be stored in a refrigerator for up to 3 weeks.

Pork & RED PEPPER CHILI

2 tablespoons olive oil
1 large onion, chopped
2 garlic cloves, crushed
1 red bell pepper, cored, seeded,
   and diced
2 cups ground pork
1 red chile, finely chopped
1 teaspoon dried oregano
2 cups strained tomatoes
13 oz can red kidney beans,
   rinsed and drained
salt and pepper

To serve
sour cream
boiled rice or crusty bread

Serves **4**
Prep time **10 minutes**
Cooking time **30 minutes**

1 Heat the oil in a saucepan, add the onion, garlic, and red bell pepper and cook for 5 minutes, or until softened and starting to brown. Add the pork and cook, stirring and breaking up the ground meat with a wooden spoon, for 5 minutes, or until browned.

2 Add all the remaining ingredients to the pan and bring to a boil. Reduce the heat and simmer gently for 20 minutes. Remove from the heat and season well with salt and pepper. Divide among serving bowls, top with a dollop of sour cream, and serve with boiled rice or crusty bread.

VARIATION
For a lamb and eggplant chili, substitute the ground pork and red bell pepper with 1 eggplant and 2 cups ground lamb. Cut the eggplant into small cubes and fry as above with the ground lamb. Garnish the finished dish with 2 tablespoons of finely chopped mint leaves and serve with boiled rice or pasta.

AFFORDABILITY 1

BEEF STEW *with* GARLIC BREAD TOPPING

1 Heat 1 tablespoon of the oil in an ovenproof casserole over high heat. Add the beef and cook for 2–3 minutes until golden. Lift out with a slotted spoon onto a plate.

2 Add the remaining oil to the pan together with the onion, carrot, and celery and cook for 5 minutes, or until softened. Stir in the tomato paste, flour, and thyme, then pour in the wine and cook for 2–3 minutes until reduced by half. Pour in the stock and simmer for 15 minutes.

3 Return the meat to the pan, season with salt and pepper, and mix well. Arrange the garlic bread slices on top of the stew. Cook under a preheated hot broiler for 3 minutes, or until the bread is golden and crisp.

2 tablespoons olive oil
13 oz beef steak, cut into chunks
1 onion, sliced
1 carrot, sliced
1 celery stalk, sliced
1 teaspoon tomato paste
2 teaspoons all-purpose flour
handful of chopped thyme
scant ½ cup red wine
scant 1 cup hot beef stock (see page 98 for homemade)
½ ready-made garlic bread baguette, sliced
salt and pepper

Serves **4**
Prep time **10 minutes**
Cooking time **30 minutes**

AFFORDABILITY 2

Creamy coconut
BEEF RENDANG

2 tablespoons vegetable oil
1 tablespoon peeled and finely
    chopped fresh ginger root
1 Thai chile, thinly sliced
1 garlic clove, thinly sliced
1 lemon grass stalk, thinly
    sliced
1 lb frying steak, cut into strips
½ teaspoon ground cinnamon
pinch of ground turmeric
juice of 1 lime
14 oz can coconut milk
4 tablespoons chopped cilantro
steamed Thai jasmine rice,
    to serve (optional)

Serves **4**
Prep time **10 minutes**
Cooking time **10 minutes**

1 Heat the oil in a large, heavy skillet or wok and cook the ginger, chile, garlic, and lemon grass over medium heat, stirring frequently, for 1-2 minutes until softened but not colored. Add the beef, increase the heat to high, and stir-fry for 5 minutes, or until browned and cooked through.

2 Stir in the cinnamon and turmeric and cook, stirring, for a few seconds before adding the lime juice and coconut milk. Gently heat, stirring, for 2-3 minutes until the sauce is hot. Serve immediately with the steamed jasmine rice, if desired, and sprinkle with the chopped cilantro.

VARIATION

For speedy Thai-style beef and coconut skewers, cut 1 lb fillet steak into chunks. Thread the steak onto 8 metal skewers alternately with 2 red bell peppers, cored, seeded, and cut into chunky pieces. Mix 4 tablespoons Thai red curry paste with scant 1 cup coconut cream in a bowl and spoon over the skewers. Cook the beef skewers under a preheated hot broiler for 3-4 minutes on each side until cooked through. Serve with warm pita bread.

AFFORDABILITY
2

PEA & LAMB KORMA

2 tablespoons olive oil
1 onion, chopped
2 garlic cloves, crushed
8 oz potatoes, cut into ¾ inch
  dice
scant 2¼ cups ground lamb
1 tablespoon korma curry
  powder
1²⁄₃ cups frozen peas
scant 1 cup vegetable stock
  (see page 15 for homemade)
2 tablespoons mango chutney
salt and pepper
chopped cilantro, to garnish

To serve
plain yogurt
steamed rice

Serves **4**
Prep time **10 minutes**
Cooking time **30 minutes**

1 Heat the oil in a saucepan, add the onion and garlic, and cook for 5 minutes, or until the onion is soft and starting to brown. Add the potatoes and lamb and cook, stirring and breaking up the lamb with a wooden spoon, for 5 minutes, or until the meat has browned.

2 Add the curry powder and cook, stirring, for 1 minute. Add the remaining ingredients and season to taste with salt and pepper. Bring to a boil, then reduce the heat, cover tightly, and simmer for 20 minutes. Divide among serving bowls, garnish with the chopped cilantro, and serve with plain yogurt and steamed rice.

STUDENT TIP

Buy rice, spices, and other ethnic ingredients from specialist stores —you'll find it's much cheaper than buying in the grocery store. If you make a lot of curries and tagines, larger jars of spices will be a lot more economical, and you can buy super-size sacks of rice and pulses that will keep your pantry stocked for weeks.

Crispy FISH PIE

butter, for greasing
1¼ cups frozen spinach
13 oz skinless salmon fillet, cubed
8 oz skinless smoked haddock fillet, cubed
4 eggs
scant ½ cup crème fraîche
2 tablespoons boiling water
⅔ cup dried bread crumbs
salt and pepper

Serves **4**
Prep time **15 minutes**
Cooking time **25 minutes**

1 Lightly grease an ovenproof dish with butter. Place the spinach in a strainer and pour over boiling water until it has defrosted. Lay the spinach on paper towels and squeeze to get rid of excess water.

2 Arrange the spinach in the prepared ovenproof dish and place the fish on top. Make 4 small hollows between the fish pieces and crack an egg into each one.

3 Mix the crème fraîche with the measured water in a mug, season to taste, and pour over the fish.

4 Sprinkle the bread crumbs over the top of the pie. Place in a preheated oven, 400°F, for 25 minutes, or until golden and bubbling and the fish is cooked through.

VARIATION

For crispy fish nuggets, cut 13 oz chunky skinless salmon fillet into small bite-size pieces. Toss the salmon with 3 tablespoons olive oil in a bowl. Place 1¼ cups dried white bread crumbs, the finely grated zest of 1 lemon, a handful of chopped parsley, and a pinch of salt in a freezer bag. Add the salmon and shake until well coated, then arrange the salmon on a lightly greased baking sheet. Drizzle with another tablespoon of olive oil, then cook under a preheated hot broiler for 5 minutes. Turn over and cook for another 2-3 minutes until golden and cooked through. Serve with a tomato salad.

FARFALLE WITH
TUNA SAUCE

4 oz can tuna in olive oil, drained
2 tablespoons extra virgin olive oil, plus extra to taste (optional)
4 tomatoes, coarsely chopped
½ cup pitted black olives, coarsely chopped
grated zest of 1 lemon
2 garlic cloves, crushed
2 tablespoons coarsely chopped parsley
11½ oz dried farfalle
salt

....

Serves **4**
Prep time **10 minutes, plus standing**
Cooking time **10 minutes**

....

1 Put the tuna in a large bowl and break it up with a fork. Stir in the oil, tomatoes, olives, lemon zest, garlic, and parsley and season with salt. Cover and let stand for at least 30 minutes (including the pasta's cooking time).

2 Meanwhile, cook the pasta in a large saucepan of salted boiling water according to the package directions until al dente. Drain well, then add to the bowl with the tuna sauce and toss to combine. Serve immediately with a drizzle of extra virgin olive oil, if desired.

COOKING TIP
To serve this dish as a pasta salad, refresh the cooked pasta in cold running water before adding the remaining ingredients.

AFFORDABILITY
1

Steamed LEMON SALMON & POTATOES

1 Set a large steamer over a saucepan of gently simmering water. Place the potatoes in the steamer and season well with salt and pepper. Cover and cook for 10 minutes.

2 Place the salmon on top of the potatoes and sprinkle around the beans. Cover and cook for another 7-10 minutes until the fish and vegetables are cooked through.

3 Meanwhile, mix together the crème fraîche, lemon zest and juice, dill, and capers in a mug and season to taste with salt and pepper. Serve the salmon and vegetables with the crème fraîche mixture.

13 oz new potatoes, sliced
2 salmon fillets
3 oz green beans, trimmed
4 tablespoons crème fraîche
finely grated zest and juice
   of ½ lemon
handful of chopped dill
1 tablespoon capers, rinsed and
   drained
salt and pepper

Serves **2**
Prep time **10 minutes**
Cooking time **20 minutes**

AFFORDABILITY
2

Smoked Haddock KEDGEREE

1 tablespoon vegetable oil
2 tablespoons butter
1 onion, finely chopped
1 garlic clove, crushed
1 teaspoon finely grated fresh
  ginger root
1 teaspoon cumin seeds
½ teaspoon coriander seeds
1 teaspoon curry powder
½ teaspoon ground turmeric
1²/₃ cups basmati rice
2¾ cups hot chicken or fish
  stock (see pages 11 or 104 for
  homemade)
10 oz skinless smoked haddock
  fillet
scant ²/₃ cup frozen peas
1 red chile, chopped
handful of chopped cilantro
salt and pepper
mango chutney, to serve

Serves **4**
Prep time **10 minutes**
Cooking time **25 minutes**

1 Heat the oil and butter in a large saucepan. Add the onion and cook for 5 minutes, then stir in the garlic and ginger and cook for 1 minute. Add the cumin and coriander seeds and cook for 30 seconds, then stir in the curry powder, turmeric, and rice and cook for another 1 minute.

2 Pour in the stock and cook for 5 minutes. Place the fish on top of the rice and cook for another 5 minutes. By this time, most of the stock should have boiled away.

3 Add the peas, cover the pan tightly with a lid, turn down the heat as low as it will go, and cook for 5-7 minutes until the rice is cooked through.

4 Use a fork to gently break up the fish, stir the fish and peas into the rice, and season to taste with salt and pepper. Sprinkle with the chile and cilantro and serve with mango chutney.

AFFORDABILITY
2

BAKED COD PARCELS
WITH BEANS & CHORIZO

4 cod fillets
13 oz can lima beans, rinsed
   and drained
¾ cup cherry tomatoes, halved
4 sprigs of thyme
4 thin slices of chorizo sausage
5 tablespoons dry white wine
salt and pepper

Serves **4**
Prep time **10 minutes**
Cooking time **15 minutes**

1 Cut 4 large sheets of parchment paper and place a cod fillet on each. Divide the beans, tomatoes, and thyme among the cod fillets.

2 Place a chorizo slice on top of each piece of fish and season well with salt and pepper, then fold the paper over and roll up the edges to create airtight packages, leaving just a little gap.

3 Pour a little wine into each parcel and then fully seal, leaving enough space in the packages for air to circulate. Place on a baking sheet and bake in a preheated oven, 425°F, for 15 minutes, or until the fish is cooked through.

VARIATION
For seared cod with bean and tomato salad, rub 1 tablespoon olive oil over 4 cod fillets and season well with salt and pepper. Place the cod, skin side down, in a preheated griddle and cook for 5 minutes. Turn over and cook for another 3 minutes, or until golden and cooked through. Meanwhile, make a dressing by whisking together 1 tablespoon balsamic vinegar and 3 tablespoons olive oil in a bowl. Toss the dressing with 1½ cups halved cherry tomatoes and a 13 oz can lima beans, rinsed and drained, 3½ oz arugula, and ½ chopped red chile and season to taste with salt and pepper. Serve the salad with the cod.

AFFORDABILITY
3

OVEN-BAKED
FISH & CHIPS
WITH TOMATO SALSA

AFFORDABILITY 2

1   Place the potatoes in a roasting pan. Drizzle over half the oil, season well with salt and pepper, and toss to make sure the potatoes are coated in oil. Bake in a preheated oven, 425°F, for 10 minutes.

2   Turn over the potatoes, place the fish on top, season again, and sprinkle over the lemon zest. Return to the oven for another 15–20 minutes until the potatoes are just cooked through.

3   Meanwhile, make the tomato salsa. Mix together the remaining oil and the vinegar in a bowl and season to taste with salt and pepper. Stir in the tomatoes, capers, and scallion.

4   Transfer the fish to serving plates, garnish with the chopped parsley, and serve with the chips and salsa on the side.

1½ lb potatoes, cut into thin
   wedges
4 tablespoons olive oil
4 skinless cod or haddock fillets
finely grated zest of 1 lemon
1 teaspoon balsamic vinegar
4 tomatoes, chopped
1 teaspoon capers, rinsed and
   drained
1 scallion, chopped
salt and pepper
handful of chopped parsley,
   to garnish

Serves **4**
Prep time **10 minutes**
Cooking time **25–30 minutes**

VARIATION
For fish fingers with sweet potato chips, toss 1½ lb sweet potatoes, peeled and cut into thin wedges, with 2 tablespoons olive oil in a roasting pan. Season to taste with salt and pepper, then bake in a preheated oven, 400°F, for 7 minutes. Meanwhile, brush 3 tablespoons mayonnaise over 13 oz skinless cod fillet, cut into fingers. Finely grate the zest of 1 lemon and mix with 1 cup dried bread crumbs on a plate. Toss the fish in the crumbs until coated. Place in the roasting pan and return to the oven for another 10 minutes, or until cooked through.

Mixed Seafood
CASSEROLE

4 tablespoons olive oil
1 onion, diced
4 garlic cloves, crushed
scant ½ cup white wine
13 oz can chopped tomatoes
scant 1 cup fish stock (see page 104 for homemade)
pinch of saffron threads
13 oz pack ready-cooked mixed seafood
2 tablespoons chopped parsley
crusty bread, to serve (optional)

Serves **4**
Prep time **5 minutes**
Cooking time **15 minutes**

1 Heat the oil in a heavy saucepan and sauté the onion and garlic for 3-4 minutes. Pour in the wine and boil for 2-3 minutes, then add the tomatoes, stock, and saffron. Bring to a simmer, stir in the mixed seafood and parsley, and cook for 5-6 minutes to heat through. Serve with crusty bread, if desired.

Buttery
SHRIMP ON TOAST

1   Place a large skillet over medium heat and melt the butter with the cayenne pepper. Once the butter begins to froth slightly, add the shrimp and cook for 2-3 minutes, stirring occasionally, until they are pink and cooked through.

2   Add the lemon juice, then stir in the chives and season to taste with salt and pepper. Spoon the shrimp and their buttery juices onto the granary toast and serve immediately.

7 tablespoons butter
pinch of cayenne pepper
10 oz raw shrimp, peeled
1 tablespoon lemon juice
2 tablespoons chopped chives
salt and pepper
4 slices of granary toast,
    to serve

Serves **4**
Prep time **5 minutes**
Cooking time **5 minutes**

STUDENT TIP

Online shopping helps to keep your budget in check, as you tend to buy what you need, rather than impulse buying in the store. You can check your spend as you add items to your cyber cart and, if you do get carried away, it's much easier to discard online items than retrace your steps in a grocery store.

STOVETOP SQUID
WITH OLIVES & TOMATOES

1 To prepare the squid, wash the tubes and pat dry on paper towels. If the tentacles are included, cut the tentacles away from the heads and wash and dry these too, discarding the heads. Cut the tubes across into thin rings.

2 Heat half the oil in a large shallow saucepan, skillet, or wok and fry the squid in two batches until they firm up into rings. Remove each batch with a slotted spoon and transfer to a plate. Set aside.

3 Add the onions to the pan or wok and fry for 3–4 minutes until the onions are beginning to color. Add the garlic and fry for another 1 minute. Return the squid and any juices on the plate to the pan or wok and add the tomatoes, olives, capers, and the remaining oil. Cook for another 2–3 minutes, stirring, until the tomatoes are hot and very slightly softened.

4 Add the lemon juice, season to taste with salt and pepper, and sprinkle with the chopped parsley. Serve with warm grainy bread or ciabatta.

COOKING TIP
Try other types of fish instead of squid. Use the same weight of cubed skinless white fish such as cod, haddock, or coley, or raw peeled shrimp.

10 oz squid tubes
4 tablespoons coconut or olive oil
2 red onions, thinly sliced
4 garlic cloves, thinly sliced
scant $1\frac{2}{3}$ cups cherry tomatoes, halved
$\frac{1}{2}$ cup pitted black olives, halved
1 tablespoon capers, rinsed and drained
2 teaspoons lemon juice
salt and pepper
3 tablespoons chopped parsley, to garnish
warm grainy bread or ciabatta, to serve

Serves **4**
Prep time **15 minutes**
Cooking time **15 minutes**

MAKE FRIENDS WITH YOUR MICROWAVE

It might sound like a luxury for student accommodation but a microwave is very affordable and worth every cent: treat it well and keep it clean and you'll be rewarded with quick and easy meals day after day. From warming the milk for your morning oatmeal to blitzing eggs, reheating leftovers, and rustling up a one-mug chocolate sponge (see opposite) for a quick sugar fix, this appliance will be one of the hardest working in the kitchen.

CHEAT'S SUPPERS

Obviously, nothing beats a homecooked meal prepared with love and attention. However, if you're dashing home between college and the bar, it's perfectly acceptable to cheat a little—especially if that means you can enjoy a hearty fresh pasta dish rather than a cheese slice wedged between a couple of pieces of bread.

- Make a personal portion of mac and cheese by half filling a very large mug or small bowl with dry macaroni. Add a pinch of salt and cover the pasta with water. Place the mug or bowl in the microwave and blitz for 2 minutes at a time, stirring in between, until the pasta is cooked (add extra water if the pasta starts to dry). Stir in a little milk and a handful of grated cheddar and microwave until the cheese is melted and has made a sauce.

- The same method applies to noodles —just use stock or sauce instead of water—and add some chopped peppers, baby corn, bean sprouts, and any other vegetables you like toward the end of the cooking time.

- If you've got a sweet tooth, you might prefer to head straight for dessert, and a chocolate microwave mug cake will certainly hit the spot. Put 4 tablespoons each of superfine sugar and self-rising flour in the largest mug you can find. Add 2 tablespoons unsweetened cocoa, mix, then add 4 tablespoons milk, a beaten egg, and a good drizzle of vegetable oil. Mix and microwave for 5 minutes, or until the cake has risen fully.

KEEP IT CLEAN

There's nothing worse that opening the door of the microwave first thing in the morning and being greeted with the festering smells of last night's dinner —or worse, the congealed remains of last night's dinner. Shared kitchens can very quickly descend into chaos with standards of hygiene and cleanliness plummeting as the semester progresses. Luckily, it's quick and easy to freshen up your microwave and all you need is a bowl and a lemon.

Pour some water into a large bowl and add the juice of half a lemon. Put the bowl in the microwave and cook for 3 minutes.

Keeping the door shut, let the bowl stand for another 5 minutes so the steam lifts off the dirt. You'll now find it's really easy to wipe the inside with a soft damp cloth.

MUSHROOM *Stroganoff* Ⓥ

1 tablespoon butter
2 tablespoons olive oil
1 onion, thinly sliced
4 garlic cloves, finely chopped
1 lb cremini mushrooms, sliced
2 tablespoons whole-grain
  mustard
1 cup crème fraîche
salt and pepper
3 tablespoons chopped parsley,
  to garnish

Serves **4**
Prep time **10 minutes**
Cooking time **10 minutes**

1 Melt the butter with the oil in a large skillet, add the onion and garlic, and cook until softened and starting to brown.

2 Add the mushrooms to the pan and cook until softened and starting to brown. Stir in the mustard and crème fraîche and just heat through. Season to taste with salt and pepper, then serve immediately, garnished with the chopped parsley.

AFFORDABILITY **1**

TOMATO & CHICKPEA STEW

Vegan

1 Heat the oil in a large heavy saucepan. Add the onion, green bell pepper, garlic, and ginger, and cook for 6-7 minutes until softened.

2 Stir in the cumin and coriander and cook for another 1 minute. Add the tomato paste, stock, tomatoes, and chickpeas, then cover and bring to a boil. Season generously with salt and pepper, reduce the heat, and simmer for 8 minutes, or until thickened slightly and the tomatoes have softened. Ladle the stew into serving bowls and serve garnished with the chopped parsley.

2½ tablespoons olive oil
1 large onion, chopped
1 green bell pepper, cored, seeded, and chopped
1 garlic clove, chopped
1 inch piece of fresh ginger root, peeled and chopped
1 teaspoon ground cumin
1 teaspoon ground coriander
2 tablespoons tomato paste
2 cups hot vegetable stock (see page 15 for homemade)
4 large tomatoes, each cut into 8 wedges
2 x 13 oz cans chickpeas, rinsed and drained
salt and pepper
2 tablespoons chopped parsley, to garnish

Serves **4**
Prep time **15 minutes**
Cooking time **20 minutes**

AFFORDABILITY
1

MUSTARDY SQUASH, CARROT & SWEET POTATO
CASSEROLE

Vegan

3 tablespoons vegetable oil

1 red onion, coarsely chopped

4 garlic cloves, chopped

1½ lb butternut squash, peeled, seeded, and cut into bite-size chunks

500 g (1 lb) sweet potatoes, peeled and cut into bite-size chunks

2 carrots, cut into bite-size chunks

½ cup dry white wine

1 teaspoon dried tarragon or rosemary

1¾ cups hot vegetable stock (see page 15 for homemade)

2 tablespoons whole-grain mustard

4 cups spinach, washed, drained, and shredded

salt and pepper

steamed couscous or rice, to serve

Serves **4**

Prep time **15 minutes**

Cooking time **30 minutes**

1 Heat the oil in a heavy saucepan. Cook the onion and garlic for 3-4 minutes until softened. Add the squash, sweet potatoes, and carrots and cook for another 3-4 minutes until lightly golden.

2 Pour in the wine, add the tarragon or rosemary, and cook until reduced by half. Add the stock and mustard to the pan, then season generously with salt and pepper, bring to a boil, and simmer gently for 15 minutes, or until the vegetables are tender.

3 Tip the spinach into the pan and stir until wilted. Serve with steamed couscous or rice.

AFFORDABILITY **1**

BROWN RICE, MINT & HALLOUMI PILAF (V)

2 tablespoons olive oil
4 oz halloumi or provolone
   cheese, cut into ½ inch
   chunks
1 large onion, chopped
1 celery stalk, chopped
2 small zucchini, diced
1 teaspoon cumin seeds
¼ teaspoon dried red pepper
   flakes
scant 1 cup brown basmati rice
3 cups vegetable stock (see
   page 15 for homemade)
¼ cup dates, chopped,
   or golden raisins (optional)
1 tablespoon chopped mint
salt and pepper

Serves **2**
Prep time **15 minutes**
Cooking time **55 minutes**

1 Heat the oil in a skillet. Add the halloumi and fry over medium heat for 3-4 minutes until the cheese is turning golden, turning the pieces a couple of times for even browning. Lift out onto a plate with a slotted spoon.

2 Add the onion, celery, and zucchini to the pan and fry for 8-10 minutes, stirring frequently, until golden. Stir in the spices and rice and cook, stirring frequently, for 1 minute.

3 Pour in the stock and bring to a gentle simmer. Reduce the heat to its lowest setting and cook for about 40 minutes, stirring frequently, until the rice is tender and all the liquid has been absorbed. Toward the end of the cooking time, pack the rice down flat with the back of the spoon so it plumps up evenly. If the mixture is dry before the rice is cooked, stir in a little hot water, but make sure all the water has cooked off so the rice is almost sticky.

4 Stir in the dates or golden raisins, if using, the halloumi and the mint. Season to taste with salt and pepper before serving.

COOKING TIP
Pilafs are remarkably versatile. You can add other vegetables like diced eggplant or bell peppers instead of the zucchini, chopped nuts or pine nuts for texture, and other herbs like cilantro or parsley. Substitute olives for the dried fruit if you prefer a more savory flavor.

Spiced
BLACK BEANS
& CABBAGE (V)

3 tablespoons butter
1 large onion, chopped
5 oz baby carrots, scrubbed
1 tablespoon ras el hanout spice
blend (see tip for homemade)
2 cups vegetable stock (see
page 15 for homemade)
7 oz new potatoes, scrubbed
and diced
13 oz can black beans, rinsed
and drained
6 oz cabbage
salt (optional)

Serves **2**
Prep time **15 minutes**
Cooking time **30 minutes**

1 Melt the butter in a saucepan and gently fry the onion and carrots for 5 minutes, or until the onion is softened. Add the spice blend and fry for another 1 minute.

2 Pour in the stock and bring to a boil. Reduce the heat to its lowest setting and stir in the potatoes and beans. Cover and cook gently for 15 minutes, or until the vegetables are tender and the juices slightly thickened.

3 Cut away the thick stalks from the cabbage and discard, then roll up the leaves and finely shred. Add to the pan and cook for another 5 minutes. Season with salt, if necessary, and serve.

COOKING TIP
For a homemade ras el hanout spice blend, place ½ teaspoon each cumin, coriander, and fennel seeds in a mortar and crush with a pestle. Add 1 teaspoon yellow mustard seeds and ¼ teaspoon each ground cinnamon and cloves and grind the spices together. Alternatively, use a small coffee or spice grinder to grind the spices.

AFFORDABILITY 1

Scrambled eggs
WITH SPINACH, GARLIC & RAISINS

1 tablespoon butter
1 shallot, chopped
1 small garlic clove, finely sliced
¼ teaspoon cumin seeds
1 tablespoon raisins
large handful of baby spinach
 leaves
2 eggs, beaten
salt and pepper
1 warm flatbread, to serve

Serves **1**
Prep time **5 minutes**
Cooking time **10 minutes**

1 Melt the butter in a small skillet or saucepan. As soon as it starts to foam, add the shallot and fry for 3 minutes to soften. Add the garlic, cumin seeds, and raisins and stir over low heat for 1 minute.

2 Add the spinach and cook until the leaves start to wilt. Immediately tip in the eggs and cook, stirring constantly, until the eggs have lightly scrambled. Season to taste with salt and pepper and serve with the warm flatbread.

COOKING TIP
Don't be put off by the unusual combination of raisins and eggs. It really works well, giving the dish a slightly Middle Eastern flavor. A pinch of ground cumin or coriander can be used instead of the seeds, and a pinch of chili is good if you like a fierier kick.

AKURI Ⓥ

AFFORDABILITY 1

1 tablespoon butter
1 small red onion, finely chopped
1 green chile, finely sliced
8 eggs, lightly beaten
1 tablespoon sour cream
1 tomato, skinned (see page 16) and finely chopped
1 tablespoon chopped cilantro
sea salt flakes
buttered toast, to serve

Serves **4**
Prep time **10 minutes**
Cooking time **10 minutes**

1 Heat the butter in a large nonstick skillet, add the onion and chile, and cook for 2-3 minutes.

2 Add the eggs, sour cream, tomato, and cilantro and season with sea salt flakes. Cook over low heat, stirring frequently, for 3-4 minutes until the eggs are lightly scrambled and set. Serve with buttered toast.

STUDENT TIP

Sign up for loyalty cards at all the big grocery stores and collect points for your shopping. You can choose to use these on your grocery bill, or swap them for vouchers or other deals. The value of points varies between retailers so check who's currently offering the best value.

Balsamic
ROAST TOMATOES

12 plum tomatoes, about
 1 lb 7 oz
2 tablespoons olive oil
2 teaspoons balsamic vinegar
small bunch of basil, leaves torn
2 tablespoons pine nuts
1 small ciabatta
salt and pepper

Serves **4**
Prep time **5 minutes**
Cooking time **40-45 minutes**

1 Halve the tomatoes and arrange, cut side uppermost, in a roasting pan. Drizzle with the oil and vinegar. Tear half the basil leaves over the top, add the pine nuts, and season with salt and pepper. Roast in a preheated oven, 350°F, for 35-40 minutes until tender.

2 Cut the ciabatta in half lengthwise then half again to give 4 quarters. Toast the cut side of the bread only, then transfer to serving plates and spoon the tomatoes on top. Tear the remaining basil leaves over the top and serve immediately.

AFFORDABILITY **1**

TARRAGON
MUSHROOM TOASTS (V)

1 Toast the brioche slices lightly and keep warm.

2 Heat the butter in a skillet and sauté the shallots, garlic, and chile, if using, for 1-2 minutes. Add the mushrooms and stir-fry over medium heat for 6-8 minutes. Season well with salt and pepper, then remove from the heat and stir in the crème fraîche and herbs.

3 Spoon the mushrooms onto the toasted brioche and serve immediately, with an extra dollop of crème fraîche, if desired.

8 slices of brioche
2/3 cup butter
2 banana shallots, finely chopped
3 garlic cloves, finely chopped
1 red chile, seeded and finely chopped (optional)
10 oz mixed wild mushrooms, such as chanterelle, cep, girolle, and oyster, or white mushrooms, trimmed and sliced
4 tablespoons crème fraîche, plus extra to garnish (optional)
2 tablespoons finely chopped tarragon
1 tablespoon finely chopped parsley
salt and pepper

Serves **4**
Prep time **15 minutes**
Cooking time **15 minutes**

AFFORDABILITY
2

Deviled
MUSHROOMS ⓥ

1 tablespoon sunflower oil
4 tablespoons butter
6 scallions, white parts finely
  chopped and green tops
  set aside
14 oz white mushrooms, sliced
2 tablespoons Worcestershire
  sauce
2 teaspoons whole-grain
  mustard
2 teaspoons tomato paste
a few drops of Tabasco sauce
  (optional)
4 slices of crusty bread
salt and pepper

Serves **4**
Prep time **5 minutes**
Cooking time **10 minutes**

1 Heat the oil and butter in a skillet. Add the white chopped scallions and the mushrooms and fry for 3–4 minutes, stirring, until golden.

2 Stir in the Worcestershire sauce, mustard, and tomato paste. Add 4 tablespoons water, the Tabasco sauce, if using, and a little salt and pepper. Cook for 2 minutes, stirring, until the sauce is beginning to thicken.

3 Toast the bread under a preheated hot broiler and arrange on serving plates.

4 Stir the green scallions tops through the mushrooms and cook for 1 minute, then spoon over the toast. Serve immediately.

AFFORDABILITY
1

CARROT & CABBAGE SLAW

AFFORDABILITY 1

1 Mix together the cabbage, carrots, scallions, yogurt, mustard, and lemon juice in a bowl and season with pepper to taste.

1²/₃ cups shredded red cabbage
2 carrots, grated
3 scallions, finely chopped
scant ½ cup plain yogurt
1 teaspoon whole-grain mustard
juice of 1 small lemon
pepper

Serves **4**
Prep time **15 minutes**

STUDENT TIP

Always check out the price per pound of the different options when you buy fruit and veg in the grocery store. You might be shocked to find that a shrink-wrapped head of broccoli or prepackaged zucchini could be up to twice the price per pound of loose vegetables.

ZUCCHINI & HERB Risotto

4 tablespoons butter
2 tablespoons olive oil
1 large onion, finely chopped
2 garlic cloves, finely chopped
scant 2 cups risotto rice
scant 1 cup white wine
6⅓ cups vegetable stock, heated to simmering (see page 15 for homemade)
4 cups baby spinach leaves, chopped
3½ oz zucchini, finely diced
¾ cup Parmesan cheese, finely grated
1 small handful of dill, mint, and chives, coarsely chopped
salt and pepper

Serves **4**
Prep time **10 minutes**
Cooking time **about 20 minutes**

1 Melt the butter with the oil in a saucepan, add the onion and garlic, and cook for about 3 minutes until softened. Add the rice and stir until coated with the butter mixture. Pour in the wine and cook rapidly, stirring, until it has evaporated.

2 Add the stock, a ladleful at a time, and cook, stirring constantly, until each addition has been absorbed before adding the next. Continue until all the stock has been absorbed and the rice is creamy and cooked but still retains a little bite—this will take around 15 minutes.

3 Stir in the spinach and zucchini and heat through for 3-5 minutes. Remove from the heat and stir in the Parmesan and herbs. Season to taste with salt and pepper and serve immediately.

AFFORDABILITY 2

BOSTON
BAKED BEANS

Vegan

1 Heat the oil in a heavy saucepan. Add the onion and cook over low heat for 5 minutes, or until softened. Add the celery and garlic and continue to cook for 1-2 minutes.

2 Add the tomatoes, stock, and soy sauce. Bring to a boil, then reduce the heat to a fast simmer and cook for about 15 minutes until the sauce begins to thicken.

3 Add the sugar, mustard, and beans and cook for another 5 minutes, or until the beans are heated through. Stir in the parsley and serve.

1 tablespoon vegetable oil
1 small red onion, finely chopped
2 celery stalks, finely chopped
1 garlic clove, crushed
¾ cup canned chopped tomatoes
⅔ cup vegetable stock (see page 15 for homemade)
1 tablespoon dark soy sauce
1 tablespoon dark brown sugar
2 teaspoons Dijon mustard
1¼ cups canned mixed beans, rinsed and drained
2 tablespoons chopped parsley

Serves **2**
Prep time **10 minutes**
Cooking time **30 minutes**

AFFORDABILITY

BRAIN BOWLS

As you're already at college or university, you must have done something right and earned your place through hard work and determination. However, there's no harm in giving your brain cells an extra boost every now and then—if nothing else, it might help to realign the balance after a few late nights on the booze. There are plenty of ingredients that will help with memory power, alertness, and general well-being and a salad is by far the easiest way to rustle up a bowl of pure brainpower.

Here are a few brain-boosting ingredients:

- Spinach (beta-carotene)
- Avocados (omega-3 fatty acid)
- Salmon, tuna, and other oily fish (essential fatty acids)
- Eggs (vitamin B12)
- Broccoli (vitamin K)
- Tomatoes (antioxidants)
- Pumpkin seeds (zinc)

QUICK SALAD IDEAS

- **Niçoise bowl** Peeled and quartered boiled egg, tomatoes, green beans, tuna, Boston lettuce, and boiled new potatoes.

- **Broccoli bowl** Steamed and cooled broccoli florets, green beans, and peas mixed with a vinaigrette dressing.

- **Something fishy bowl** Steamed and cooled salmon fillet on a bed of baby spinach, sprinkled with pumpkin seeds, and drizzled with balsamic vinegar and olive oil.

- **Cool as a cucumber bowl** Cubed avocado, cucumber, tomatoes, and feta cheese mixed with a drizzle of olive oil and lemon juice. For a heartier meal, add some chopped, cooked chicken breast.

SOUPER SUPPER

Soup is another quick and easy way to rustle up a bowl of intelligence-boosting food. You can create a delicious, warming soup from virtually any ingredients and it's a particularly good way to use up leftover meat or vegetables (as long as they've been kept in the refrigerator). For example, leftover potatoes, sweet potato, squash, carrots, spinach, or broccoli can be gently heated in a little stock or water and then blitzed with a handheld blender for an almost instant lunch. Sprinkle some health-giving seeds on your soup before serving.

Tomatoes also make an excellent base for soups and the addition of garlic, fresh basil, and plenty of seasoning will make it a bowl of comfort food that's hard to beat.

Basic PIZZA DOUGH

¼ oz fresh yeast or
   1 teaspoon dried yeast
pinch of superfine sugar
3¾ cups all-purpose flour, plus
   extra for dusting
1½ cups lukewarm water
1½ teaspoons salt
olive oil, for oiling

Serves **4**
Prep time **20 minutes, plus
   standing, resting and
   rising**

1 Dissolve the yeast in a bowl with the sugar, 2 tablespoons of the flour, and 3½ tablespoons of the measured water. Let stand for 5 minutes until it starts to form bubbles.

2 Add the remaining water, the salt, and half the remaining flour and stir with one hand until you have a pastelike mixture. Gradually add all the remaining flour, working the mixture until you have a moist dough. Shape the dough into a ball, cover with a moist dishtowel, and let rest in a warm place for 5 minutes.

3 Lightly dust a counter with flour and knead the dough for 10 minutes, or until smooth and elastic. Shape into 4 equal-size balls and place, spaced apart, on a lightly oiled baking sheet. Cover with a moist dishtowel and let rise in a warm place for 1 hour. Use according to your recipe.

AFFORDABILITY
1

BASIC TOMATO SAUCE

Vegan

1 Heat the oil in a heavy saucepan over medium heat. Add the garlic and cook for 30 seconds, stirring, then add the tomatoes, sugar, and basil, if using. Season lightly with salt and bring to a boil.

2 You now have two options. If you want a very light sauce to spoon over stuffed fresh pasta or if your sauce will be used in another recipe where it will undergo further cooking, simmer the sauce over medium heat for 2-3 minutes. Alternatively, if you are aiming for a more robust, concentrated tomato sauce to stir into pasta, simmer the sauce over low heat for 40-45 minutes until thick and rich. The sauce can be eaten chunky or blended with a handheld blender until smooth, then reheated.

2 teaspoons olive oil
1 garlic clove, finely chopped
5 cups canned chopped tomatoes
large pinch of superfine sugar
5 basil leaves (optional)
salt

Serves **8**
Prep time **5 minutes**
Cooking time **5 minutes (for a light sauce), 45-50 minutes (for a robust sauce)**

AFFORDABILITY 1

EASY LAMB & BARLEY RISOTTO

SLOWLY DOES IT

CHICKEN & SWEET POTATO
WEDGES

JERK PORK WITH PINEAPPLE SALSA

MONDAY SAUSAGE STEW

BAKED SEAFOOD
WITH PAPRIKA

CHICKEN & CARAMELIZED ONION DHAL

1. Heat the oil in a large saucepan and fry the onions for 8-10 minutes, stirring frequently until deep golden. Using a slotted spoon, transfer half of the onions to a plate and set aside.

2. Add the urad dhal to the pan with the stock, garlic, ginger, turmeric, and cumin seeds. Bring to a gentle simmer and let cook, stirring frequently, for 1-1¼ hours until the lentils are tender and the mixture has a thick, souplike consistency. If it starts to dry out, add a little water. Stir in the chicken and cook gently for 10 minutes.

3. Season to taste with plenty of pepper. Divide among serving bowls, spoon the reserved onions on top, and garnish with chopped cilantro. Serve with lemon or lime wedges and warm flatbreads.

COOKING TIP
Urad dhal is most widely available in health food and Indian stores. Red or black lentils can be used instead but these cook more quickly, so reduce the stock to 3 cups and cook the lentils until tender, topping off with water if the mixture starts to dry out.

3 tablespoons vegetable oil
3 onions, chopped
1 cup urad dhal, rinsed
4 cups chicken or vegetable stock (see pages 11 or 15 for homemade)
2 garlic cloves, finely chopped
¾ oz fresh ginger root, peeled and finely chopped
1 teaspoon ground turmeric
1 teaspoon cumin seeds
10-13 oz boneless, skinless chicken breast, cut into large pieces
pepper
coarsely chopped cilantro, to garnish

To serve
lemon or lime wedges
warm flatbreads

Serves **4**
Prep time **15 minutes**
Cooking time **1½-1¾ hours**

AFFORDABILITY
2

CHICKEN & SWEET POTATO
wedges

4 sweet potatoes, about 2½ lb
in total, scrubbed and cut
into thick wedges
4 boneless, skinless chicken
thighs, cut into chunks
1 red onion, cut into wedges
4 plum tomatoes, cut into
chunks
5 oz chorizo sausage, skinned
and sliced or diced,
if very large
leaves from 3 sprigs of
rosemary
4 tablespoons olive oil
salt and pepper
watercress salad, to serve
(optional)

Serves **4**
Prep time **20 minutes**
35 minutes

1 Put the sweet potatoes in a large roasting pan with the chicken, onion, and tomatoes. Tuck the chorizo in and around the sweet potatoes, then sprinkle with the rosemary and some salt and pepper. Drizzle with the oil.

2 Roast in a preheated oven, 400°F, for about 35 minutes, turning once or twice, until the chicken is golden and cooked through and the sweet potato wedges are browned and tender. Spoon onto serving plates and serve with a watercress salad, if desired.

VARIATION
For mixed roots with fennel and chicken, use a mixture of 2½ lb baking potatoes, parsnips, and carrots. Scrub the potatoes and peel the parsnips and carrots, then cut the root vegetables into wedges. Add to the roasting pan with the chicken as above. Sprinkle with 2 teaspoons fennel seeds, 1 teaspoon ground turmeric, and 1 teaspoon paprika, then drizzle with 4 tablespoons olive oil and roast as above.

AFFORDABILITY 1

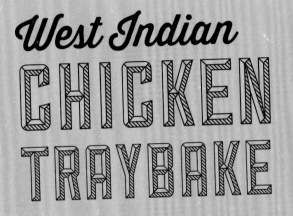

West Indian CHICKEN TRAYBAKE

AFFORDABILITY 2

3 tablespoons vegetable or mild olive oil
2 onions, sliced
2 red bell peppers, cored, seeded, and sliced
2 teaspoons paprika
1 teaspoon ground cumin
4 garlic cloves, finely chopped
2 lb skinless, boned chicken thighs
1¼ cups chicken or vegetable stock (see pages 11 or 15 for homemade)
14 oz can coconut milk
6 fresh or frozen mini corn cobs
4 tomatoes, cut into chunks
salt and pepper
chopped cilantro, to garnish
warm cornbread, to serve (see page 61 for homemade)

Serves **6**
Prep time **20 minutes**
Cooking time **1¾ hours**

 1 Heat 2 tablespoons of the oil in a roasting pan on the stove and gently fry the onions and red bell peppers for 10 minutes, stirring frequently, until golden. Stir in the spices and garlic. Add the remaining oil and the chicken thighs to the pan, turning them in the spicy mixture until lightly seared.

2 Add the stock and then the coconut milk, stirring the ingredients to combine. Push the corn cobs down into the liquid and bring to a gentle simmer.

3 Cover with foil and bake in a preheated oven, 350°F for 1¼ hours.

4 Stir in the tomatoes and return to the oven, uncovered, for another 15 minutes. Season to taste with salt and pepper and garnish with the chopped cilantro. Serve with the warm cornbread.

COOKING TIP
Stir in scant 1½ cups frozen corn instead of the corn cobs if preferred. This is a dish to put on the center of the table and let everyone help themselves. Serve with plenty of bread for mopping up the juices.

BALSAMIC BRAISED
PORK CHOPS

4 spare rib pork chops, about
  1½ lb in total
3 tablespoons balsamic vinegar
2 tablespoons light brown
  sugar
2 onions, thinly sliced
2 dessert apples, peeled, cored,
  and quartered
2 tablespoons cornstarch
3 teaspoons English mustard
scant 1 cup boiling chicken
  stock (see page 11 for
  homemade)
chopped chives, to garnish
  (optional)

To serve
mashed potatoes
steamed Brussels sprouts

Serves **4**
Prep time **15 minutes**
7-8 hours

1 Preheat the slow cooker if necessary; see the manufacturer's directions. Arrange the pork chops in the bottom of the slow cooker pot and spoon over the vinegar and sugar. Sprinkle the onions on top, then add the apples.

2 Put the cornstarch and mustard in a mug and blend with a little cold water to make a smooth paste, then gradually stir in the stock until smooth and pour over the pork. Cover with the lid and cook on high for 30 minutes. Reduce the heat and cook on low for 6½-7½ hours until the pork is cooked through and tender.

3 Transfer the pork to serving plates, stir the sauce, and spoon over the chops. Sprinkle with chopped chives, if desired. Serve with mashed potatoes and steamed Brussels sprouts.

VARIATION
For a cider-braised pork, prepare the pork chops as above, omitting the vinegar. Bring scant 1 cup hard cider to a boil in a saucepan. Make up the cornstarch paste as above, then gradually stir in the boiling cider instead of the stock. Pour over the chops and continue as above.

Easy
LAMB & BARLEY
RISOTTO

¾ oz mixed dried mushrooms
4 cups boiling vegetable stock
  (see page 15 for homemade)
4 tablespoons cream sherry
  or fresh orange juice
1 onion, finely chopped
1 teaspoon ground cumin
2 garlic cloves, finely chopped
¼ cup golden raisins
scant ¾ cup pearl barley
4 lamb chump chops, about
  5 oz each
8 oz pumpkin or butternut
  squash, peeled, seeded, and
  cut into ¾ inch dice
salt and pepper
chopped mint and parsley,
  to garnish
harissa, to serve

Serves **4**
Prep time **15 minutes**
7-8 hours

1 Preheat the slow cooker if necessary; see the manufacturer's directions. Put the dried mushrooms in the slow cooker pot, pour in the stock, then stir in the sherry or orange juice, onion, cumin, garlic, golden raisins, and barley and season with salt and pepper. Arrange the chops on top in a single layer, season with salt and pepper, then tuck the pumpkin or squash into the gaps between the chops. Press the chops and pumpkin or squash down lightly into the stock, then cover with the lid and cook on low for 7-8 hours until the lamb and vegetables are tender.

2 Lift the chops out of the slow cooker and break them into pieces. Stir the risotto well, then spoon onto serving plates, top with the chops, and garnish with the chopped herbs. Serve with spoonfuls of harissa, if desired.

VARIATION
For a pumpkin & barley risotto, omit the lamb and use 3½ cups diced pumpkin. Cook as above, then add 2½ cups spinach to the risotto for the last 15 minutes of the cooking time. Serve topped with spoonfuls of Greek yogurt, chopped fresh mint and parsley, and buttery fried slivered almonds.

AFFORDABILITY 3

MONDAY SAUSAGE STEW

1 lb pork chipolatas
1 onion, chopped
2 x 13½ oz cans baked beans
2 tablespoons Worcestershire
    sauce
1 teaspoon dried mixed herbs
1 teaspoon Dijon mustard
scant 1 cup boiling chicken
    stock (see page 11 for
    homemade)
10 oz pumpkin or butternut
    squash, peeled, seeded, and
    cut into ¾ inch cubes
salt and pepper
garlic bread, to serve (optional)

Serves **4**
Preparation time **25 minutes**
Cooking time **7-8 hours**

1 Preheat the slow cooker if necessary; see the manufacturer's directions. Broil the sausages on one side only.

2 Put the onion, baked beans, and Worcestershire sauce in the slow cooker pot. Stir in the herbs, mustard, and stock, then mix in the pumpkin or squash. Season with salt and pepper. Arrange the sausages on top, browned sides uppermost, and press them into the liquid. Cover with the lid and cook on low for 7-8 hours until the sausages are cooked through and the pumpkin or squash is tender. Spoon into shallow serving bowls and serve with garlic bread, if desired.

VARIATION
For a chillied sausage stew, broil 1 lb chilied pork sausages or plain chipolatas. Put the onion and 2 x 13½ oz cans mixed beans in chili sauce in the slow cooker pot, omitting the Worcestershire sauce, dried herbs, and Dijon mustard. Mix in the stock and pumpkin or squash and cook as above. Garnish with 3 tablespoons chopped parsley.

AFFORDABILITY 1

SPICY PULLED HAM
with apricots

1½ lb smoked ham joint, well
   rinsed with cold water
1¼ cups apple or orange juice
¾ inch piece of fresh ginger
   root, peeled and grated, or
   1 teaspoon ground ginger
2 tablespoons sweet chili sauce
1 tablespoon brown sugar
6 fresh apricots, halved and
   pitted

To serve
6 seeded baps
3½ oz watercress or arugula

Serves **6**
Prep time **10 minutes, plus
   standing**
Cooking time **4½ hours**

1 Put the ham in a small roasting pan or baking
dish and add the fruit juice. Cover with foil and bake
in a preheated oven, 325°F, for 4 hours, turning the
ham over about halfway through the cooking time.

2 Combine the ginger, chili sauce, and sugar in a mug and
spread over the top of the ham. Arrange the apricots
around the meat, turning them in the fruit juice.

3 Return to the oven, uncovered, for another 30 minutes
until the glaze is stickily coating the meat and the
apricots are tender. Let stand for 10 minutes.

4 Transfer the ham to a board and shred the meat away
from the joint using a fork.

5 To serve, halve the baps and drizzle a tablespoonful
of the cooking juices over the bases. Sandwich the baps
together with the watercress or arugula, apricots, and
shredded ham. Serve warm.

COOKING TIP
If you don't have time to cook and serve the ham on the
same day, slow-cook it a day in advance, cool, and chill
overnight before finishing in a hot oven with the sticky
glaze. Just make sure it's hot right through to the center
when you serve it. If you're not serving 6, chill the ham
in the refrigerator for several days and use up in salads,
snacks, and sandwiches.

AFFORDABILITY
2

Jerk PORK
WITH PINEAPPLE SALSA

1½–1¾ lb pork shoulder joint
2 tablespoons powdered jerk
   spice mix
4 teaspoons light brown sugar
1 onion, coarsely chopped
1 carrot, sliced
scant 1 cup boiling chicken
   stock (see page 11 for
   homemade)
salt and pepper
boiled rice, to serve (optional)

Pineapple salsa
1 small pineapple, skinned,
   cored, and finely chopped
2 teaspoons light brown sugar
1 large red chile, halved, seeded,
   and finely chopped
grated zest of 1 lime

Serves **4**
Prep time **20 minutes**
5-6 hours

1 Preheat the slow cooker if necessary; see the manufacturer's directions. Remove the string from the pork, then cut away the skin. Unroll and, if needed, make a slit in the meat so that it can be opened out to make a strip that is of an even thickness. Rub the pork all over with the jerk spice mix, sugar, and salt and pepper. Put the pork in the slow cooker pot, then sprinkle the onion and carrot into the gaps around the pork. Pour in the stock, cover with the lid, and cook on high for 5-6 hours until the meat is very tender and almost falls apart.

2 Meanwhile, put the pineapple in a bowl with the sugar, chile, and lime zest. Mix together, then cover with plastic wrap and chill until the pork is ready.

3 Lift the pork out of the slow cooker pot, remove any fat, then shred the meat with 2 forks. Serve with the salsa and boiled rice, if desired.

AFFORDABILITY
2

PORK BELLY
& NAPA CABBAGE WRAPS

1 large onion, sliced
1 large fennel bulb, sliced
2 lb lean pork belly, skinned
1½ teaspoons fennel seeds
1 teaspoon Chinese five-spice
  powder
½ napa cabbage, about
  11½ oz, very thinly sliced
4 white or whole-wheat wraps
4 tablespoons Asian plum
  sauce or hoisin sauce

Serves **4**
Prep time **10 minutes,
  plus standing**
Cooking time **4 hours**

1 Sprinkle the onion and fennel slices in a small roasting pan. Lay the piece of pork on top with the fattiest side uppermost. Sprinkle evenly with the fennel seeds and five-spice powder.

2 Cover with foil and bake in a preheated oven, 300°F, for 4 hours, or until the meat is very tender, uncovering the pan for the last hour. Remove from the oven and lift the meat out of the pan. Tilt the pan so all the juices collect in one corner. Use a tablespoon or serving spoon to skim off the fat, leaving the meaty juices in the pan. Stir the cabbage into the juices, return the meat to the pan, and leave in a warm place to stand for 10 minutes.

3 Meanwhile, lightly broil the wraps under a preheated hot broiler until warmed through.

4 Transfer the meat to a board and slice as thinly as possible. Spread the center of each wrap with plum or hoisin sauce, then sprinkle the shredded cabbage over the sauce and arrange the pork and cooked vegetables on top. Roll up and serve warm.

TURKEY & HAM CASSEROLE

1 Season the flour with a little salt and pepper on a plate. Cut the turkey into small chunks and coat with the seasoned flour.

2 Melt the butter in an ovenproof casserole and fry the turkey for 5 minutes, or until golden on all sides. Add the onions and celery to the casserole and fry for 4–5 minutes until softened. Tip in any remaining flour left on the plate. Pour in the stock, add the thyme and chili powder, and bring to a simmer, stirring.

3 Cover the casserole and cook in a preheated oven, 350°F, for 45 minutes.

4 Stir the sweet potatoes and ham into the casserole and return to the oven for another 30 minutes. Stir in the cranberries and crème fraîche and season to taste with salt and pepper. Return to the oven for a final 15 minutes before serving.

2 tablespoons all-purpose flour
1¼ lb turkey breast meat
3½ tablespoons butter
2 onions, chopped
2 celery stalks, sliced
3 cups chicken stock (see page 11 for homemade)
1 tablespoon chopped thyme
½ teaspoon mild chili powder
10 oz sweet potatoes, scrubbed and cut into small chunks
11½ oz ready-cooked ham in one piece, cut into dice
1½ cups cranberries
scant ½ cup crème fraîche
salt and pepper

Serves **6**
Prep time **20 minutes**
Cooking time **1¾ hours**

AFFORDABILITY
2

THREE MEALS
THREE WAYS

There are a number of recipes that you can cook that will open the door to a veritable smorgasbord of culinary treats. This is like multitasking to the extreme—you're essentially creating a number of different dishes while cooking one meal, and with just a few tweaks you can transform today's pasta sauce into tomorrow's pizza topping. The trick is to cook two or even three times, the amount you need for today's meal and then portion up the remainder to be used the following day, or frozen for another time entirely. We've started you off with a few ideas below.

BOLOGNESE SAUCE

1 Obviously for your first meal, you use this deliciously rich, meaty sauce as an accompaniment for pasta—be that the traditional spaghetti, or penne, fusilli, etc.

2 Use the second portion as a lasagna sauce. Technically, this is still one-pot cooking as the sauce is already prepared and you're cooking the lasagna in just one dish. Simply spoon a layer of sauce on the bottom of the dish, arrange a layer of lasagna sheets on top, and then cover with some white sauce—repeat three times for a sturdy lasagna that doesn't run away over the plate. Bake in a preheated oven, 350°F, for about 30 minutes.

3 For chili con carne, add 1 teaspoon chili powder and a drained and rinsed can of red kidney beans to the third portion of sauce. Heat thoroughly and serve with boiled rice.

ROAST CHICKEN

1 Transform your Sunday roast into a Monday curry: add a little oil to a pan with a chopped onion and fry until softened. Add 1/2 teaspoon each of ground turmeric, ground coriander, and chili powder and stir in a 400 g (13 oz) can of chopped tomatoes. Cook for a few minutes then stir in chopped leftover cooked chicken and cook for about 10 minutes. Finish with a swirl of yogurt or crème fraîche.

2 Shred some of the leftover cooked chicken, mix together in a bowl with some chopped scallion, red bell pepper, and cucumber and soy sauce. Use this mixture to fill wontons or wraps for a healthy lunch.

3 Make a superquick chicken Caesar salad by mixing together coarsely chopped leftover cooked chicken, cos lettuce, and shavings of Parmesan cheese in a bowl. Serve with ranch dressing and croutons— and anchovies, if you have a jar in the pantry.

PULLED PORK

1 This is the perfect meal to prepare for a dinner party or summer lunch with friends as you can serve the same dish a number of different ways at the same time. Firstly, shred some of the meat, mix with a potent barbecue sauce, and serve in warmed buns—delicious.

2 Next, pile some pork and chopped peppers and chilies into warmed tacos for a Mexican-inspired take on the classic dish.

3 Finally, spread out a couple of pizza bases, spoon over strained tomatoes and torn mozzarella, and sprinkle some shredded pork on top before cooking.

FEIJOADA
WITH STICKY RIBS

1 tablespoon vegetable or mild olive oil
½ cup coarsely diced smoked lean bacon
2 red onions, coarsely chopped
3 garlic cloves, finely chopped
1 green chili, seeded and finely chopped
2 x 13 oz cans black beans, rinsed and drained
2 cups chicken or vegetable stock (see pages 11 or 15 for homemade)
7 oz can chopped tomatoes
1 tablespoon red or white wine vinegar
1 lb pork ribs, sold as individual ribs or in one piece
2 tablespoons light or dark brown sugar
½ teaspoon paprika
salt and pepper

Serves **3-4**
Prep time **15 minutes**
Cooking time 1**½ hours**

1. Heat the oil in a large, shallow ovenproof casserole. Add the bacon and onions and fry gently for 5 minutes, stirring frequently, until the onions are beginning to color. Add the garlic and chili and fry for another 1 minute.

2. Stir in the beans, stock, tomatoes, 1 teaspoon of the vinegar, and a little salt and pepper and bring to a boil. Reduce the heat slightly and cook for 10-15 minutes, stirring frequently, until the liquid has thickened to make a thick sauce.

3. If the pork ribs are in one piece, cut them into 3 or 4 rib pieces. Place the ribs on top of the stew. Combine the sugar with the paprika and the remaining vinegar and spoon half over the ribs, spreading it with the back of a teaspoon.

4. Cover the casserole and bake in a preheated oven, 325°F, for 30 minutes. Remove the lid and spread the pork with the remaining paprika mixture. Return to the oven, uncovered, for another 45 minutes.

AFFORDABILITY
2

Beef & coconut
STEW

1 tablespoon all-purpose flour
  or cornstarch
¼ teaspoon ground turmeric
1 lb diced braising beef
2 tablespoons vegetable or
  mild olive oil
1 large onion, chopped
1 green bell pepper, cored,
  seeded, and thinly sliced
2 teaspoons yellow mustard
  seeds
1 teaspoon fenugreek seeds
  (optional)
8-10 cardamom pods
¼ teaspoon dried red pepper
  flakes
4 garlic cloves, finely chopped
14 oz can coconut milk
salt and pepper
chunks of bread or boiled
  basmati rice, to serve

Serves **4**
Prep time **20 minutes**
Cooking time **1½-1¾ hours**

1 On a dinner plate, mix together the flour or cornstarch, turmeric, and a little salt and pepper. Add the beef and turn in the flour mixture until coated.

2 Heat 1 tablespoon of the oil in a large saucepan. Add half the beef and fry quickly for 3-4 minutes, stirring, until browned. Lift out of the pan with a slotted spoon and return to the plate. Add the remaining beef and cook for 3-4 minutes, stirring, until browned, then transfer the beef to the plate.

3 Add the remaining oil to the pan with the onion and green bell pepper and fry gently for 4-5 minutes. Return the beef to the pan with any excess flour on the plate. Add the spices and garlic and cook for 2 minutes. Add the coconut milk and heat until barely simmering. Cover and cook very gently for about 1¼-1½ hours until the beef is very tender. Take care not to boil the meat or it'll make it tough.

4 Season to taste with salt and pepper. Divide among serving bowls and serve with chunks of bread or boiled basmati rice.

AFFORDABILITY **2**

1 onion, finely chopped
1 red bell pepper, cored, seeded,
   and diced
2 garlic cloves, finely chopped
13 oz can chopped tomatoes
2/3 cup dry white wine or fish
   stock (see page 104
   for homemade)
large pinch of paprika
2 sprigs of thyme
1 tablespoon olive oil
13 oz package frozen seafood
   (shrimp, mussels, squid),
   defrosted
salt and pepper
chopped parsley, to garnish
cooked pasta, such as
   tagliatelle, to serve

Serves **4**
Preparation time **15 minutes**
Cooking time **5½–7½ hours**

BAKED
SEAFOOD
WITH PAPRIKA

1 Preheat the slow cooker if necessary; see the manufacturer's directions. Put the onion, red bell pepper, garlic, and tomatoes into the slow cooker pot, then add the wine or stock, paprika, thyme, oil, and a little salt and pepper. Cover with the lid and cook on low for 5–7 hours.

2 Rinse the seafood with cold water, drain, and then stir into the slow cooker pot. Cover again and cook on high for 30 minutes, or until piping hot. Garnish with the chopped parsley and serve with cooked pasta.

STUDENT TIP

It might sound obvious, but don't wait until you're ready to cook to check you have all the ingredients needed for a recipe. Go through the pantry in the morning so you can pick up any missing items while you're out and about.

SWEET STUFF & DRINKS

SUMMER FRUIT GRATIN

CHOCOLATE FUDGE BROWNIE

SYRUP SPONGE PUDDING

TROPICAL FRUIT SMOOTHIE

Bircher MUESLI Ⓥ

1 Mix together the buckwheat flakes, milk, apple juice, and apple in a bowl. Cover with plastic wrap and let soak overnight.

2 To serve, stir the honey, dried fruit, and nuts into the muesli mixture. Spoon into serving bowls, then top with the poached or canned fruit.

VARIATION
You can try this recipe with any of your favorite dried fruit and nuts or you can add a bit of dried coconut for a tropical flavor.

generous 1 cup buckwheat flakes
1¼ cups milk
scant ½ cup apple juice
1 apple, peeled and grated

To serve
2 tablespoons honey
⅔ cup ready-to-eat dried fruit, such as mango, apricots, or golden raisins
¾ cup hazelnuts, toasted and coarsely chopped
poached or canned fruit, such as peaches or berries

Serves **4**
Prep time **5 minutes, plus overnight soaking**

BUCKWHEAT OATMEAL

generous 1 cup buckwheat
  flakes
1 ripe banana, chopped
½ teaspoon ground cinnamon
½ cup golden raisins
scant 1 cup milk
scant 1 cup water

To serve
honey
scant 1½ cups mixed berries

Serves **4**
Prep time **5 minutes**
Cooking time **5 minutes**

1 Place all the ingredients in a saucepan over low heat and bring to a simmer, then cook gently for 3-4 minutes until the buckwheat flakes are tender.

2 Blend briefly with a handheld blender, then spoon into serving bowls, drizzle with a little honey, and serve with mixed berries.

VARIATION
Replace the banana with a chopped pear and serve with chopped toasted walnuts and honey.

STUDENT TIP

When it comes to shopping for everyday items, a quick and easy way to save money is to switch from big brands to own brands. Breakfast cereals, condiments, drinks, and cleaning products are just some of the own-brand shopping-cart staples that will slash your budget.

PUMPKIN SEED & APRICOT
Muesli Ⓥ

½ cup jumbo rolled oats
1 tablespoon golden raisins or raisins
1 tablespoon pumpkin seeds
1 tablespoon chopped almonds
2 tablespoons chopped ready-to-eat dried apricots
2 tablespoons fruit juice, such as apple or orange juice, or water
2 small apples, peeled and grated
3 tablespoons milk or plain yogurt, to serve

Serves **2**
Prep time **5 minutes**
Cooking time **5 minutes**

AFFORDABILITY
2

1 Place the oats, golden raisins or raisins, pumpkin seeds, almonds, and apricots in a bowl with the fruit juice or water. Add the apple and mix well. Spoon into serving bowls and serve topped with milk or yogurt.

STUDENT TIP

Whether you're lucky enough to have a dishwasher or you have to get down and dirty with the dishes, always rinse pots, pans, and plates as soon as they've been used. That way, if the dishwashing fairies turn up late for their shift, the food won't have dried like a layer of cement and clearing up will be easier.

BAKED HONEY
PEACHES ⓥ

3½ tablespoons butter, plus
  extra for greasing
4 large peaches, halved and
  pitted
scant ⅔ cup slivered almonds
¼ cup honey
ground cinnamon, for dusting
sour cream, to serve

Serves **4**
Prep time **5 minutes**
Cooking time **10-15 minutes**

1 Grease a shallow baking dish with butter. Place the
peaches, skin side down, in the prepared baking dish.
Dot the peaches with butter, then sprinkle with the
almonds, drizzle with the honey, and dust with a
little cinnamon.

2 Bake in a preheated oven, 400°F, for 10-15 minutes
until the peaches are start to color and the almonds
have lightly browned. Serve the peaches with the
juices drizzled over, and topped with a spoonful of
sour cream.

AFFORDABILITY
1

RHUBARB & GINGER SLUMP Ⓥ

1½ lb rhubarb, trimmed and cut into chunks
1 tablespoon self-rising flour
¼ cup granulated sugar
2 pieces of preserved ginger in syrup, drained and chopped, plus 2 tablespoons syrup from the jar

Topping
¾ cup self-rising flour
⅓ cup butter, softened
6 tablespoons granulated sugar
4 tablespoons milk
1 egg, beaten

Serves **4-6**
Prep time **10 minutes**
Cooking time **30 minutes**

AFFORDABILITY
2

1 Place the rhubarb, flour, sugar, chopped ginger, and syrup in a shallow ovenproof dish and toss together. Cover with foil and place in a preheated oven, 375°F, for 3 minutes.

2 Meanwhile, make the topping. Place all the ingredients in a food processor and blend until smooth. Alternatively, rub the butter into the dry ingredients with your fingertips and then stir in the milk and beaten egg.

3 Uncover the rhubarb and spoon over the topping. Return to the oven for another 25 minutes, or until the topping is golden and cooked through.

VARIATION
For rhubarb and ginger fools, whip scant 1 cup heavy cream until soft peaks form, then stir in 1 tablespoon confectioners' sugar. Gently stir in 4 oz canned rhubarb, drained and chopped, and divide among serving bowls. Crumble 1 ginger cookie over each portion and serve immediately.

APPLE & SALTED CARAMEL
Pudding  Ⓥ

4 large tart dessert apples,
   such as Cox's
1 tablespoon lemon juice
5 tablespoons raw brown sugar
4 oz ready-made caramel sauce
¼ teaspoon sea salt flakes
3½ tablespoons unsalted
   butter, very soft
4 thick slices white bread,
   crusts removed
pouring cream or ice cream,
   to serve

Serves **4**
Prep time **20 minutes**
Cooking time **40 minutes**

1 Peel, core, and slice the apples. Put the apples in a pie dish, add the lemon juice and 2 tablespoons of the sugar, and mix the ingredients together. Cover with foil and bake in a preheated oven, 375°F, for 30 minutes until the apples are very tender.

2 Drizzle the caramel sauce over the apples with a teaspoon so it's fairly evenly distributed. Pinch the sea salt flakes between your fingers to crumble them up and sprinkle over the caramel.

3 Generously butter the bread slices with half the butter. Cut into triangles and arrange over the filling, buttered side up. Sprinkle with the remaining sugar and dot with the remaining butter.

4 Bake for another 10 minutes, uncovered, until the bread is crisped and heated through. If you like, pop the dish under a preheated hot broiler for a few minutes until the surface is deep golden, but watch closely as it will quickly toast! Serve with pouring cream or ice cream.

AFFORDABILITY 2

CHOCOLATE FUDGE BROWNIE Ⓥ

¾ cup + 2 tablespoons butter
7 oz semisweet chocolate, chopped
¾ cup packed soft dark brown sugar
¾ cup superfine sugar
4 eggs, beaten
½ cup ground almonds
9 tablespoons all-purpose flour
vanilla ice cream, to serve (optional)

Serves **8**
Prep time **10 minutes, plus cooling**
Cooking time **30 minutes**

1 Melt the butter and chocolate in a shallow ovenproof dish, about 9 inches across, over low heat. Remove from the heat and let cool for a couple of minutes.

2 Beat together the sugars and eggs in a bowl, then stir in the chocolate mixture followed by the almonds and flour.

3 Wipe the rim of the ovenproof dish with a damp piece of paper towel to neaten, then pour in the chocolate batter. Bake in a preheated oven, 350°F, for 25 minutes, or until just set. Serve warm with ice cream, if desired.

AFFORDABILITY
2

SYRUP SPONGE
Pudding Ⓥ

1 Grease a 5 cup ovenproof dish with butter. Place all the ingredients, except the corn syrup, in a food processor and blend until smooth. Spoon 4 tablespoons of the corn syrup into the bottom of the prepared dish, then add the mixture and smooth the surface with a knife.

2 Cover with microwave-proof plastic wrap and pierce the wrap a couple of times with a sharp knife. Cook in a microwave oven on medium heat for about 12 minutes. Test to see if it is cooked by inserting a skewer into the pudding; it should come out clean.

3 Let rest for 3 minutes, then turn out onto a deep plate and spoon over the remaining corn syrup. Serve with cream or custard.

¾ cup butter, softened, plus extra for greasing
¾ cup superfine sugar
1⅓ cups self-rising flour
1 teaspoon baking powder
3 eggs
1 teaspoon vanilla extract
3 tablespoons milk
finely grated zest of ½ lemon
6 tablespoons light corn syrup
cream or custard, to serve

Serves **6**
Prep time **5 minutes, plus resting**
Cooking time **15 minutes**

Prune CLAFOUTIS

butter, for greasing
3 eggs
2/3 cup superfine sugar
6 tablespoons all-purpose flour
2/3 cup heavy cream
2/3 cup milk
1 teaspoon vanilla extract
2/3 cup pitted soft prunes

Serves **4**
Prep time **10 minutes**
Cooking time **20-25 minutes**

AFFORDABILITY
2

1 Lightly grease a shallow ovenproof dish with butter. Whisk together the eggs and sugar in a bowl until pale, frothy, and tripled in volume. Sift the flour into the bowl and lightly fold in. Add the cream, milk, and vanilla extract and mix until just combined.

2 Pour into the prepared ovenproof dish and bake in a preheated oven, 375°F, for 5 minutes, or until the surface is just starting to set. Sprinkle over the prunes, then return to the oven for another 15-20 minutes until the clafoutis is risen and golden.

CRUNCHY BERRY Brûlée

1 cup mascarpone cheese
1¼ cups ready-made fresh custard
1 cup mixed berries
½ cup superfine sugar
1½ tablespoons water

Serves **4**
Prep time **5 minutes**
Cooking time **15 minutes**

1 Beat the mascarpone in a bowl until smooth. Gently stir in the custard. Transfer the mixture to a serving dish and sprinkle the berries over the top.

2 Place the sugar and measured water in a small heavy saucepan and slowly bring to a boil, carefully swirling the pan from time to time. Keep cooking until the sugar dissolves, then turns a deep caramel color. Pour over the berries and leave for a few minutes to harden.

VARIATION

For a melting berry yogurt, place 1⅓ cups mixed berries in a serving dish. Spoon over 1¼ cups plain yogurt, then sprinkle with ⅓ cup packed soft dark brown sugar. Chill in the refrigerator for 20–25 minutes until the sugar has melted.

AFFORDABILITY 2

PASSION FRUIT & MANGO MESS

1 Whip the cream with the confectioners' sugar in a bowl until it just holds its shape.

2 Gently stir in the meringue, most of the mango, and a little of the passion fruit pulp. Spoon into glasses and top with the remaining fruit.

VARIATION
For a passion fruit and mango cream, peel, seed, and chop 1 mango and divide among 4 glasses. Whisk 1 egg yolk with 2 tablespoons superfine sugar in a bowl until very frothy and pale, then stir in the pulp of 2 passion fruit. Whip scant 1 cup heavy cream in a separate bowl until soft peaks form, then stir into the egg mixture and whisk until thickened. Gently stir in 1 tablespoon orange liqueur and 3 oz crushed meringues. Spoon over the mango and top with a little more chopped fruit, if desired.

1¼ cups heavy cream
2–3 tablespoons confectioners' sugar
4 meringue nests, crushed
1 mango, peeled, seeded, and sliced
1 passion fruit, halved

Serves **4**
Prep time **10 minutes**

AFFORDABILITY
1

Crunchy PEAR CRUMBLE

1. Place the pears in a shallow ovenproof dish with the sugar, cinnamon, and measured water and stir together. Cover with foil and place in a preheated oven, 375°F, for 5 minutes.

2. Meanwhile, make the crumble topping. Place the sugar in a food processor with the cinnamon, oats, flour, and butter and pulse until the mixture resembles fine bread crumbs. Alternatively, rub the butter into the dry ingredients with your fingertips. Stir the corn syrup into the topping mixture.

3. Remove the pears from the oven, uncover and sprinkle the topping over them. Return to the oven for another 20-25 minutes until bubbling and lightly browned. Serve warm with custard.

VARIATION

For sautéed pears with crunchy topping, heat 2 tablespoons butter in a skillet. Add 6 pears, peeled, quartered, and cored, and cook for 5 minutes, turning often, until golden all over. Stir in ½ teaspoon ground cinnamon and 6 tablespoons orange juice and cook until the liquid bubbles away. Divide among serving bowls, then sprinkle with 6 crushed oat cookies mixed with scant ¼ cup chopped pecans. Spoon over plain yogurt or whipped cream to serve.

6 pears, peeled, cored, and chopped
2 tablespoons soft light brown sugar
½ teaspoon ground cinnamon
4 tablespoons water
custard, to serve

Topping
⅓ cup packed soft light brown sugar
½ teaspoon ground cinnamon
1⅓ cups rolled oats
9 tablespoons all-purpose flour
⅓ cup butter
1 tablespoon light corn syrup

Serves **6**
Prep time **10 minutes**
Cooking time **25-30 minutes**

AFFORDABILITY 1

ONE-POT ENTERTAINING

Entertaining at home doesn't have to entail long days sweating in the kitchen, arranging napkins into intricate shapes, and trying to rustle up a matching 64-piece bone china dinner service. You can make it as laid back and low key as you like—after all, many students survive college on a diet of beans on toast, caffeine, and alcohol so no one is going to judge your cooking or hosting skills too harshly. However, you probably want everyone to enjoy the meal so it's a good idea not to attempt a brand-new recipe when you're entertaining eight people. Choose something you've made before and are confident cooking; that way you can relax and enjoy the evening too.

One-pot entertaining has a number of obvious benefits—less clutter on the worktops, less clearing up, and much less chance of spectacular failure. It's harder to overcook or burn a one-pot meal, as you just have the one dish to think about, plus you tend to add all—or most of—the ingredients at the same time, so there's less chance of forgetting something vital and spoiling the meal.

Don't forget to check if anyone is vegetarian: if they are, you'll need to decide whether to cook a meat-free meal or cook something different for your veggie mates. Likewise, if anyone has food allergies, intolerances—or is just plain fussy—it's better to find out before you're about to serve dinner.

TOP TIPS FOR A TOP NIGHT

- Plan ahead—check the timings for preparation and cooking and make sure you have the right amount of each ingredient.

- Buy a few nibbles or some bread and dips to serve as an appetizer. This will take the pressure off you when you're cooking.

- Don't forget to preheat the oven so it's at the right temperature when you're ready to start cooking.

- Are you serving sides or bread with the meal? Don't forget to prepare these so they're ready at the same time as the main course.

- Check meat and fish are cooked through thoroughly before serving —you don't want to give your mates food poisoning.

- Create a playlist for the evening. That way, you won't have to get up and change the music in the middle of the meal.

- Check you have enough plates, cutlery, and glasses well in advance.

- If you only have a small refrigerator, use a cool box and some ice packs for storing drinks—refrigerator space for the food.

ROAST PLUMS
WITH STAR ANISE Ⓥ

1 lb plums
⅛ teaspoon ground cinnamon
   or ginger
1 tablespoon broken star anise
   pieces
3 tablespoons raw brown sugar
2 teaspoons lemon juice
3½ tablespoons unsalted butter
vanilla ice cream, to serve

Serves **4**
Prep time **5 minutes**
Cooking time **20 minutes**

1 Halve and pit the plums and arrange, cut sides face up, in a shallow ovenproof dish or roasting pan.

2 Using your fingers, sprinkle the cinnamon or ginger over the plums. Arrange the star anise pieces on top, breaking them further if the pieces are fairly intact so you have enough for most of the plums.

3 Sprinkle with the sugar and then drizzle with the lemon juice. Dot a small piece of butter onto each plum. Pour 3 tablespoons water into the dish or pan.

4 Bake in a preheated oven, 400°F, for about 20 minutes until the plums are just tender. The time will vary depending on the ripeness of the plums. Divide the plums among serving plates and drizzle with the pan juices. Serve with vanilla ice cream.

AFFORDABILITY
1

BANANA CARAMEL
Puffs

1 Heat the sugar and measured water in a large ovenproof skillet until golden and caramel colored. Carefully add the butter and swirl around the pan until melted.

2 Meanwhile, cut out 4 circles from the pastry using a 3 inch cookie cutter or glass.

3 Carefully arrange the banana slices in 4 circles in the caramel, then place a pastry circle on top of each. Place in a preheated oven, 425°F, for 15 minutes, or until the pastry is puffed and cooked through. Use a spatula to turn out of the pan and drizzle with the remaining sauce.

VARIATION

For banana and caramel pots, slice 2 bananas and divide among serving bowls. Whisk $2/3$ cup heavy cream in a bowl until soft peaks form, then stir in 1 tablespoon dulce de leche or other caramel sauce. Spoon over the banana, then drizzle with more dulce de leche and top with chopped pecans.

$2/3$ cup packed soft light brown sugar
$3\frac{1}{2}$ tablespoons water
2 tablespoons butter
10 oz ready-rolled puff pastry
2 bananas, sliced

Serves **4**
Prep time **5 minutes**
Cooking time **25 minutes**

SWEET AVOCADO CREAM
with mixed berries

3 large ripe avocados
finely grated zest and juice
    of 1 lime
scant ½ cup superfine sugar
3 tablespoons light cream
1 egg white
mixed fresh berries, such as
    blackberries and raspberries,
    to decorate

Serves **4**
Prep time **10 minutes, plus
    chilling**

1 Halve and pit the avocados and scoop the flesh into
a food processor or blender. Add the lime zest and juice
and half the sugar and blend to a smooth puree. Blend
in the cream.

2 Whisk the egg white in a thoroughly clean bowl until
peaking. Gradually whisk in the remaining sugar, a
teaspoonful at a time. Stir the egg white mixture gently
into the avocado puree and spoon into serving dishes.
Chill in the refrigerator. When you are ready to serve,
divide among serving bowls and sprinkle the berries
on top.

COOKING TIP
If you don't have a blender or food processor, mash the
avocado as smoothly as possible with a potato masher before
stirring in the cream. It's easiest to mash the avocados on
a flat plate or in a pan. This will only work if the avocados are
properly ripe.

Creamy CHOCOLATE PUDDING

6 tablespoons granulated
   sugar
3 tablespoons cornstarch
¼ cup unsweetened cocoa
3 eggs
2 cups milk
3 oz milk chocolate, chopped

To serve
whipped cream
grated milk chocolate

Serves **4**
Prep time **10 minutes, plus
   freezing**
Cooking time **10 minutes**

1 Place the sugar, cornstarch, and cocoa in a heatproof bowl
and whisk in the eggs. Bring the milk to a boil in a saucepan,
then whisk a little of it into the egg mixture. Transfer the
cocoa mixture to the saucepan, stir well, and cook for
3-5 minutes, stirring continuously, until thickened.

2 Place the chopped chocolate in the bowl, strain the
chocolate custard on top, and stir until smooth. Cover the
surface with plastic wrap to prevent a skin forming, then
place in the freezer for 15 minutes, stirring occasionally,
until cool.

3 When the chocolate custard is cool, divide among serving
bowls, top with whipped cream, and sprinkle with grated
chocolate.

VARIATION
For creamy chocolate truffles, bring 5 tablespoons heavy
cream to a boil in a small heavy saucepan. Place 5 oz chopped
semisweet chocolate in a heatproof bowl with 2 tablespoons
butter. Pour over the cream and stir until smooth. Place in the
freezer for 15 minutes, stirring occasionally, until the mixture
has set. Use a teaspoon to scoop out pieces of the mixture,
form into balls, and roll in cocoa to serve.

AFFORDABILITY 1

PEACH & RASPBERRY Melba Ⓥ

1 Place the measured water, sugar, and vanilla extract in a saucepan, cook over low heat, until the sugar dissolves, then cook over high heat for 5-10 minutes until syrupy.

2 Add the peach halves and cook for another 5 minutes, or until tender, then let cool. Remove the skins and thinly slice the peaches.

3 Arrange the peach slices, ice cream, and half the raspberries in sundae glasses. Press the remaining raspberries through a strainer set over a bowl to make a coulis. Drizzle the coulis over the top of the sundaes and serve with cookie curls.

VARIATION

For baked peaches and raspberries, place 4 halved and pitted peaches in an ovenproof dish. Pour over 6 tablespoons orange juice and add 2 tablespoons orange liqueur, if desired. Dot a little butter on each peach, then sprinkle with 2 tablespoons superfine sugar. Place in a preheated oven, 400°F, for 15 minutes, then sprinkle over scant 1 cup raspberries and return to the oven for another 3 minutes, or until the peaches are tender and lightly caramelized. Serve with vanilla ice cream.

1 cup water
2/3 cup superfine sugar
1 teaspoon vanilla extract
4 peaches, halved and pitted
8 scoops of vanilla ice cream
1 cup raspberries
cookie curls, to serve

Serves **4**
Prep time **5 minutes, plus cooling**
Cooking time **10-15 minutes**

WHITE CHOCOLATE
RISOTTO WITH RASPBERRIES

V

1 Put the milk in a large saucepan and heat gently until it starts to rise up in the pan. Add the rice and vanilla extract and reduce the heat to its lowest setting.

2 Stirring almost continuously, cook the risotto for about 15-20 minutes until the consistency is creamy and the rice is tender but retains a little bite. If the rice starts to dry out before the rice is cooked, add a dash more milk or water. As soon as the rice is cooked, remove the pan from the heat.

3 Break 3 oz of the chocolate into pieces and stir into the rice until it's melted. Stir in half the raspberries until they're warmed through in the heat of the rice. Spoon into small serving bowls and sprinkle the remaining raspberries on top. Grate the remaining chocolate on top to serve.

VARIATION
Try other fruits such as sliced strawberries, blueberries, or blackberries instead of the raspberries.

generous 1¾ cups milk
⅔ cup risotto rice
1 teaspoon vanilla extract
3½ oz white chocolate
1¼ cups raspberries

Serves **4**
Prep time **20 minutes**
Cooking time **15-20 minutes**

AFFORDABILITY
2

CHOC CHIP ICE CREAM *Sandwiches*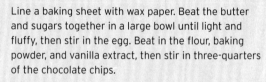

²⁄₃ cup butter, softened
½ cup granulated sugar
scant ½ cup packed soft light
   brown sugar
1 egg, beaten
1⅓ cups all-purpose flour
1 teaspoon baking powder
1 teaspoon vanilla extract
3½ oz mixed semisweet, milk,
   and white chocolate chips
4 scoops of vanilla ice cream

Serves **4 (with leftover cookies)**
Prep time **10 minutes, plus cooling**
Cooking time **10 minutes**

1   Line a baking sheet with wax paper. Beat the butter and sugars together in a large bowl until light and fluffy, then stir in the egg. Beat in the flour, baking powder, and vanilla extract, then stir in three-quarters of the chocolate chips.

2   Use a teaspoon to dollop 24 walnut-size balls of dough, well spaced apart, onto the prepared baking sheet and flatten gently. Sprinkle with the remaining chocolate chips and cook in the preheated oven, 375°F, for 8–10 minutes until golden and just cooked through.

3   Let the cookies cool on a wire rack, then serve 2 cookies to each person, sandwiched together with a scoop of vanilla ice cream.

AFFORDABILITY 2

TIRAMISU

scant 1 cup heavy cream
3½ tablespoons Marsala wine
1 cup mascarpone cheese
4 tablespoons confectioners'
  sugar
1 teaspoon vanilla extract
1¼ cups very strong coffee,
  cooled
20 ladyfingers
1 oz semisweet chocolate,
  grated, to decorate

....
Serves **4**
Prep time **15 minutes, plus
  chilling**
....

1 Whip the cream in a bowl until stiff peaks form. Set aside 1 tablespoon of the Marsala, then stir the remaining Marsala into the cream with the mascarpone, 3 tablespoons of the confectioners' sugar, and the vanilla extract.

2 Stir the remaining Marsala and confectioners' sugar into the coffee, then dip 4 of the ladyfingers into the mixture and place each in the bottom of a glass or small serving dish. The ladyfingers should be just soft, not soggy.

3 Spoon some of the creamy mixture on top, then repeat the layers to use up the remaining ingredients. Chill in the refrigerator for 20 minutes, then serve sprinkled with grated chocolate.

AFFORDABILITY **3**

STUDENT TIP

Student freezers are often filled with more ice than food. Don't wait until you can't shut the door: a regular defrost will help the freezer run more economically and maximize the storage space. This is a great revision-avoidance job.

SUMMER FRUIT GRATIN

1 Arrange all the fruit in a shallow ovenproof dish. Mix the mascarpone in a bowl with 2 tablespoons of the sugar, the cream, and lime zest, then spoon over the fruit and spread into an even layer. Sprinkle the top with the remaining sugar.

2 Place the ovenproof dish on a baking sheet and bake in a preheated oven, 375°F, for 15 minutes, or until the cheese has softened and the sugar topping has caramelized. Serve immediately.

VARIATION
For a tropical fruit gratin, arrange slices of 1 large mango in the dish with 1 sliced papaya and 1 cup blueberries. Top with the mascarpone mix and bake as above.

2 peaches, halved, pitted, and sliced
4 red plums, halved, pitted, and sliced
1¼ cups mixed raspberries and blackberries (or all raspberries)
scant 1 cup mascarpone cheese
4 tablespoons superfine sugar
2 tablespoons heavy cream
grated zest of 1 lime

Serves **4**
Prep time **10 minutes**
Cooking time **20 minutes**

AFFORDABILITY
2

MANGO CRUMBLE CHEESECAKE

1 Using a wooden spoon, beat the cream cheese in a bowl with the sugar and vanilla extract until softened. Add the eggs to one side of the bowl and tilt the bowl so you can beat the eggs to break them up thoroughly before combining them with the cream cheese. Beat in 1 teaspoon of the lime juice.

2 Turn into a shallow ovenproof dish—a small pie dish is ideal. Stand the dish in a roasting pan and pour a ¾ inch depth of boiling water into the roasting pan. (Using the roasting pan and boiling water isn't essential but it helps bake the cheesecake evenly and stops it drying out around the edges.) Bake in a preheated oven, 325°F, for 25-30 minutes until the cheesecake is lightly set around the edges but is still very wobbly in the center.

3 While cooking, halve the mangoes either side of the flat seed. Cut away the skin and dice the flesh. Sprinkle the mango over the cheesecake and drizzle with the remaining lime juice. Crumble the cookies on top and sprinkle with the slivered almonds.

4 Return to the oven, in the roasting pan, for another 10 minutes until the topping is lightly cooked. Serve warm, dusted with confectioners' sugar, if desired.

2 cups whole cream cheese
⅓ cup superfine sugar
1½ teaspoons vanilla extract
2 eggs
1 tablespoon lime juice
1 large or 2 small ripe mangoes
3 oz crumbly oat or ginger cookies
3 tablespoons toasted slivered almonds
confectioners' sugar, for dusting (optional)

Serves **4-5**
Prep time **10 minutes**
Cooking time **35-40 minutes**

Hot Caribbean
FRUIT SALAD

3½ tablespoons unsalted butter
scant ¼ cup packed light brown sugar
1 large papaya, halved, seeded, peeled and sliced
1 large mango, peeled, seeded, and sliced
½ pineapple, skinned, cored, and cut into chunks
14 oz can coconut milk
grated zest and juice of 1 lime

Serves **4**
Prep time **15 minutes**
Cooking time **10 minutes**

1   Melt the butter in a large skillet, add the sugar, and heat gently until just dissolved. Add all the fruit and cook for 2 minutes, then pour in the coconut milk and lime juice and add half the lime zest. Heat gently for 4–5 minutes, then serve warm in shallow serving bowls, sprinkled with the remaining lime zest.

CARDAMOM COFFEE

3 tablespoons strong, freshly ground coffee (South Indian, Colombian, or Javan)
1 teaspoon crushed cardamom seeds
1 cup milk
2 tablespoons sugar
2½ cups water

Serves **4**
Prep time **5 minutes**
Cooking time **5 minutes**

1 Place the coffee, cardamom seeds, milk, sugar, and measured water in a large saucepan and bring to a boil. Reduce the heat and simmer for 1-2 minutes.

2 Using a very fine-meshed strainer lined with cheesecloth, strain the coffee into mugs and serve hot.

LEMONGRASS TEA

Vegan

3-4 lemon grass stalks, finely chopped
4 teaspoons Indian tea leaves (Darjeeling or Assam)
3 cups water

To serve
milk
sugar

Serves **4**
Prep time **5 minutes**
Cooking time **5 minutes**

1 Put the lemon grass and tea leaves in a large saucepan with the measured water and bring to a boil. Reduce the heat and simmer, uncovered, for 2-3 minutes.

2 Using a fine-meshed strainer lined with cheesecloth, strain the tea into mugs. Serve hot, adding milk and sugar to taste.

Hot spiced ALMOND MILK

Vegan

1¼ cups unsweetened almond milk or other nut milk
½ cinnamon stick
2 cloves
½ teaspoon vanilla extract
maple syrup, or soft brown sugar, to taste

To serve (optional)
ice cubes
freshly grated nutmeg

Serves **1**
Prep time **5 minutes, plus infusing**
Cooking time **5 minutes**

1 Pour the milk into a small saucepan, add the cinnamon and cloves, and heat gently to almost boiling point, then turn off the heat and let infuse for at least 15 minutes, or overnight in the refrigerator.

2 Remove and discard the spices, then stir in the vanilla extract and maple syrup or sugar to taste. Reheat if serving warm, or serve cold or chilled over ice. Sprinkle over a little nutmeg, if desired.

AFFORDABILITY **1**

TROPICAL FRUIT *Smoothie* 🖤 *Vegan*

1 Place all the ingredients in a food processor or blender and blitz until smooth. Pour into 4 glasses and serve immediately.

1 mango, peeled, seeded, and chopped
2 kiwifruits, peeled and chopped
1 banana, cut into chunks
14 oz can pineapple chunks or pieces in natural juice
generous 1¾ cups orange or apple juice
handful of ice cubes

Serves **4**
Prep time **10 minutes**

AFFORDABILITY
2

YOGURT & BERRY *Smoothie* Ⓥ

1 Place all the ingredients in a food processor or a blender and blitz until smooth. Pour into 4 glasses, decorate with a few extra whole berries, and serve immediately.

1¼ cups plain yogurt
3½ cups fresh or frozen mixed summer berries, defrosted if frozen, plus extra to decorate
4 tablespoons millet flakes
3 tablespoons honey
1¼ cups cranberry juice

Serves **4**
Prep time **5 minutes**

INDEX

Acknowledgments

123RF.com 5second 165; akulamatiau 20; Baloncici 21a; foodandmore 183; hamik 21c; Hiromichi Koike 164; Joshua Resnick 21b, 148; Maxim Shebeko 182; oeytoja 82; Olena Danileiko 83; PaylessImages 205r; yelenayemchuk 164; Yulia Davidovich 205l.

Octopus Publishing Group 65al, 109; David Munns 169al, 171; Emma Neish 28, 110, 166; Ian Garlick 122, 158; Ian Wallace 41, 51, 60, 65b, 84, 85, 97, 98, 107; Lis Parsons 10, 14, 26, 38, 48, 55, 57, 69, 73, 74, 90, 123b, 127, 130, 145; Stephen Conroy 2bl, 9b, 16, 22, 52, 65ar, 66, 70, 81, 83a & c, 87, 91, 92, 102, 123ar, 133, 134, 136, 137, 150, 162, 168, 169br, 173, 175, 187; Will Heap 27, 39, 40, 43, 44, 45, 89, 95, 101, 106, 111, 114, 115, 117, 118, 119, 121, 129, 159, 189al, 215, 217; William Reavell 146, 151, 152; William Shaw 2 a & br, 9al & ar, 11, 12, 15, 17, 19, 24, 25, 29, 31, 32, 33, 35, 36, 47, 49, 53, 56, 58, 59, 61, 62, 63, 64, 67, 71, 72, 75, 77, 78, 80, 94, 96, 99, 103, 104, 105, 112, 113, 123al, 125, 126, 128, 131, 135, 139, 141, 142, 143, 144, 155, 169 ar & bl, 176, 179, 181, 189 ar, bl & br, 190, 194, 197, 198, 199, 200, 201, 203, 207, 209, 210, 213, 214, 219a & b.

Publisher Sarah Ford
Extra recipes by Joanna Farrow
Features writer Cara Frost-Sharratt
Editor Natalie Bradley
Copy Editor Clare Churly
Proofreader Jane Birch
Indexer Isobel McLean
Senior Designer Jaz Bahra
Designer Jeremy Tilston
Production Controller Meskerem Berhane